ELIZABETH I

Michael Palmer

B.T. BATSFORD LTD, LONDON

Typeset by Tek-Art Ltd, Kent
and printed in Great Britain by
The Bath Press
Bath
for the publishers
B.T. Batsford Ltd
4 Fitzhardinge Street
London W1H 0AH

ISBN 0 7134 5660 4

Acknowledgments
The Author and Publisher would like to thank the
following for permission to reproduce illustrations:
Mary Evans Picture Library for pages 9, 13, 16, 19, 25,
29, 31, 32, 38, 43, 47, 50, 51, 55; John Freeman & Co. for
pages 6, 15, 24, 26, 34, 40, 41, 42, 53, 54; A.F. Kersting
for page 57; The Mansell Collection for pages 17, 18, 23,
27, 33, 39, 46, 52, 58, 59; The Walker Art Gallery for the
frontispiece. All other illustrations are from the
collection of the Publisher.

Frontispiece *Elizabeth. Portrait attributed to Nicholas
Hilliard, 1575.*

Cover Illustrations (clockwise from top left): *Elizabeth
I in Parliament* (Publisher's collection); *Elizabeth I* by M.
Gheeraerts the Younger (courtesy National Portrait
Gallery); *The Knighting of Sir Francis Drake on board the
Golden Hind in 1581* (courtesy Mary Evans Picture
Library); Elizabeth of Tilbury in 1588 (courtesy John
Freeman & Co.); *Engraving of Elizabeth I,* after Sir Isaac
Oliver, by William Rogers (Publisher's collection).

Contents

Time Chart

1533 (7 Sept)	Elizabeth born.
1558 (17 Nov)	Queen Elizabeth comes to the throne.
1559	Acts of Supremacy and Uniformity passed. Treaty of Cateau Cambrésis.
1560	Treaty of Edinburgh signed.
1562	Elizabeth nearly dies of smallpox.
1565	Marriage of Mary and Darnley.
1567	Murder of Darnley.
1568	Mary Queen of Scots escapes to England. Incident at St Jean d'Uloa. Elizabeth borrows Philip II's bullion.
1569	Rebellion of the Northern Earls.
1570	The Bull of Excommunication published.
1571	Discovery of the Ridolfi Plot.
1572	The Treaty of Blois. The execution of the Duke of Norfolk. The Massacre of St Bartholomew.
1576	The Pacification of Ghent.
1579	Elizabeth flirts with Francis of Anjou.
1580	Drake completes circumnavigation voyage.
1583	Whitgift becomes Archbishop of Canterbury.
1584	The Duke of Anjou dies. William the Silent assassinated.
1585	Leicester's expedition to the Netherlands.
1586	Babington Plot discovered.
1587	Mary Queen of Scots executed. Drake's attack.
1588	Defeat of the Spanish Armada.
1589	The Portugal expedition.
1595	The last expedition of Hawkins and Drake.
1596	Essex's Cadiz expedition.
1598	Lord Burghley dies.
1601	The Monopolies debate. The Earl of Essex executed.
1603 (24 Mar)	Queen Elizabeth dies.

The Reputation

Elizabeth, the Virgin Queen

The glamorous figure of Queen Elizabeth dazzled her contemporaries and has found legions of admirers ever since her death in 1603. Few have doubted that she was a woman of forceful personality and great political ability; and her achievement has seemed all the more impressive by contrast with the failures of her Stuart successors James I and Charles I, under whom the monarchy was discredited and England drifted into civil war. During the Queen's lifetime, courtiers, poets and ballad-makers paid her honours usually reserved for a goddess, and her accession to the throne on 17 November 1558 was celebrated as a day of national thanksgiving from 1569 until the end of the eighteenth century.

Most later historians continued to admire her, but with a shift of

Garter procession. Elizabeth is being carried in a raised chair by her courtiers. The nobles in front reveal their garters and the beautifully dressed womenfolk follow behind. Famous people are willing to perform the menial task of carrying the Queen.

emphasis. For two centuries Elizabeth was regarded as the Protestant Heroine who saved England from the evils of Catholicism, personified by her sister and predecessor, 'Bloody' Mary, and by the woman who might have supplanted her, Mary Queen of Scots. But with the growth of religious tolerance, historians have been more inclined to praise Elizabeth's religious moderation and play down the anti-Catholic aspects of her reign. Even a durable reputation such as Elizabeth's is evidently subject to change, and merits investigation.

On examination, most people's ideas about the Queen turn out to be a mixture of facts and images. The best known fact about her is that she led England to victory over Spain, thanks to the defeat of the Spanish Armada by her navy. She is seen as a queen who presided over a united England, in which her people admired her for her dedication to the nation and to the Protestant Church. And an important element in her image is her brilliant court, which contributed to the artistic success of the age by patronising artists, poets and musicians.

The courtiers of Elizabeth's reign included such men as Sir Walter Raleigh (1552-1618) and Sir Philip Sidney (1554-1586).

Elizabeth is also famous for her role as 'the Virgin Queen'. As such she features in many romantic novels, whose authors have been intrigued by her supposedly stoical control over her emotions. In speculating about how far her heart entered into her relationships with her courtiers and suitors, they tend to forget that her beauty, her eligibility and her ability to bear children must have begun to decline by the time she reached 35, the normal life expectancy of the time. Since she reached this age in 1568, the legend of her youth and maidenhood can be viewed as a charade for most of her reign, or at any rate as a propaganda exercise.

There is no doubt that Elizabeth was assisted by a propaganda machine which sought to emphasize her youth and vigour, as well as her domination over her subjects. Other English monarchs had recognized the need to be

The 'rainbow' portrait of Elizabeth. There is much symbolism in this picture. Her cloak is covered with eyes and ears, a serpent on her arm indicates intelligence and the rainbow in her hand symbolizes peace. This portrait is at Hatfield House, the home built by Robert Cecil, who may have commissioned it. It shows a very young Elizabeth for a painting which dates from 1600.

seen to be stronger and wealthier than their great nobles and to emphasize this by splendid, lavish displays. These were even more effective if powerful people were seen to be performing menial tasks in the presence of the monarch, implicitly affirming his or her superiority.

Effective propaganda was even more important to Elizabeth than to previous male monarchs. It should not be forgotten that the English had little experience of being ruled by a woman. Queen Maud had held power in the twelfth century for only a few months; in the sixteenth, Queen Mary Tudor reigned for four years. No one knew whether the image of a glamorous court was enough to uphold a Queen's authority, especially as she grew older. There was therefore some point in creating the impression that the Queen was ageless, if not immortal. Her reputation as the Virgin Queen was helpful in this respect, as it made Elizabeth seem different from other people, especially if she was projected not as a nun in a nunnery, but as a Faery Queen in a classical Golden Age. This image of the Queen came through particularly in poetry and song. Edmund Spenser was encouraged by the courtier, Sir Walter Raleigh, to write *The Faery Queen*, the longest poem in the English language. Elizabeth appears in it under a number of different names, a peculiarity that is explained by Spenser in the poem.

Ne let his fairest Cynthia refuse
In mirrours more than one her selfe to see
But either Gloriana let her chuse
Or in Belphoebe fashioned to be
In th'one her rule, in th'other her faire chastitee.

Cynthia (Raleigh's preferred name for Elizabeth) will be called Gloriana as the ruler and Belphoebe as the chaste beauty. Thomas Morley, a gentleman of the Chapel Royal with a monopoly of music-printing, commissioned 26 composers to contribute madrigals dedicated to Elizabeth for a collection called *The Triumphs of Oriana*. Oriana was Elizabeth, the Queen goddess, and each madrigal ended with the words, 'Then sang the shepherds and nymphs of Diana, Long live fair Oriana.' Diana was the classical goddess of hunting.

The same kind of mythic image was conveyed through portraiture. Elizabeth was painted as she wanted to be seen, not as she was. Painters were instructed to work from a model face of the Queen which had no light and shade and therefore would show no wrinkles. Sir Walter Raleigh wrote that many portraits of her had to be broken up and burned for not coming up to what was required. Extravagant clothing, similar in style, always enveloped the rest of the body except for the hands and feet. What remained was the glorified Queen, aged about 35, and the main difference between one painting and another were the symbols included to highlight some flattering aspect of Elizabeth's character and achievement.

This kind of image-making became more frequent as the reign went on, presumably because it seemed increasingly important to bolster or maintain the Queen's authority. The historian may well ask what this was intended to hide.

This is even more important in view of the impact of the Queen's court, which was considered to be one of the most magnificent in Europe. A Dutch diplomat recorded that he had never met such fine instrumental music, a better pack of greyhounds or richer accoutrements on horsemen as those he saw at Eltham Palace. A German visitor was very impressed in 1598 by the public display in the Presence Chamber when the Queen processed to Chapel accompanied by her Court. Every Sunday morning the public were

---

Raleigh managed to flatter both Queen Elizabeth and Spenser in the verse he wrote to preface *The Faerie Queen*

If Chastitie want ought,
    or Temperaunce her due
Behold her Princely mind aright,
    and write thy Queene anew.
Meanwhile she shall perceive how far
    her virtues soar
Above the reach of all that live,
    or such as wrote of yore;
And thereby will excuse and favour
    thy good will:
Whose virtue can not be expressed,
    but by an Angel's quill
Of me no lines are lov'd,
    nor letters are of price,
Of all which speak our English tongue,
    but those of thy device.

Thomas Morley (1557-1603) was a famous composer of Elizabeth's reign. He worked as organist of St Paul's Cathedral, but his fame rests on his madrigals and church music.

Processed: walked in procession.

permitted to see this and to stay on for the ceremonial laying of the royal table. When the German, Hentzner, was there, the public were also allowed to present petitions to her, which occasioned the acclamation 'Long Live Queen Elizabeth' and her answer 'Thank you my good people'.

The court was a mobile institution travelling from palace to palace in the vicinity of London. In the summer it would go further afield towards the Midlands and the West Country (but never to the North or Wales) on what was known as a progress. An elaborate procession would travel along a carefully prepared route, visiting towns and staying in the country houses of the Queen's peers. Elaborate entertainments would be laid on lasting

A medal commemorating the Armada together with Elizabeth's very flowery signature. The writing reads Elizabeth by the Grace of God (D.G.) Queen (REG) of England (ANGLIE), France (F) and Ireland (HI). Compare the inscription on a coin of Elizabeth II and ask yourself which of Queen Elizabeth's titles has been left out. Also why is Elizabeth Queen of France?

The 'Ditchley' portrait of Elizabeth. Elizabeth stands on the Oxfordshire part of the map of England published by Saxton in 1583. The Queen is shown as the Princess of Light while the storm gathers. The poem reads:
The prince of Light. The Sun by whom
things live,
Of heaven the glory and of earth the Grace,
Hath no such glory as you grace to give
Where Correspondence will have no place.

Progress to Elvetham, 1591. Elizabeth had a three-day stay at the home of the Earl of Hertford. Before she and the court arrived the house was enlarged, outbuildings were constructed for her entourage and a half moon pond with islands was constructed. Three days of entertainment were arranged for the Queen's amusement. After Nereus (with a cornered cap) came five Tritons breast high in the water . . . and all five cheerfully sounded their trumpets.

several days, such as those at Elvetham, arranged by the Earl of Hertford in 1591.

What was remarkable about Elizabeth was that she could communicate a caring, sympathetic image through all this display. She was able to suggest a concern for the problems her subjects were facing. At the beginning of her reign Sir John Hayward wrote in his Annals of the First Four Years of Queen Elizabeth 'If ever a person had either the gift or style to win the hearts of the people it was the Queen and ever she did express the same, it was at present, in coupling mildness with majesty as she did and in stately stooping to the meaner sort.' This quality of charm and intellect was a powerful weapon in maintaining people's allegiance and loyalty, whether they were ministers and courtiers, or the mayors of towns.

Whatever people's misgivings about a woman ruler, there is no doubt that Elizabeth possessed the ultimate authority in the state, and that she had a personality strong enough to control her ministers. Her reputation as a ruler is that she was moderate and conservative. It is said that she came to the throne intent upon finding a system that would please the maximum number of people and, having found it, she perpetuated and defended it. Her Church Settlement has been interpreted as the discovery of a middle way between Protestant and Catholic extremes within which she was prepared to tolerate diversity of opinion. She is also seen as someone who was more merciful than her Inquisitor sister, Mary Tudor, and than most of her advisers, whose religious views tended more to one extreme or the other. As we shall see, these views can and have been challenged.

Inquisitor: an officer of the Inquisition, a tribunal for the punishment of heresy.

Her conservatism was displayed in her attitude to parliament. She used it as little as possible and might not have called it at all, but for her dependence on parliament for money. She and her Privy Council used a number of expedients to control parliamentary business when it did meet and the Queen was adept at stopping any attempt by parliament to dictate policy to her. She would listen to these petitions but answer them with the maximum evasiveness and she was very quick to use her veto. Her regime was therefore very narrowly based upon her Court and Privy Council. It is proper to wonder whether she would have held the allegiance of most of her people if the Spanish invasion threat had not loomed to make those who felt left out and ignored consider that national unity was more important than their own aspirations. There were enough signs of the collapse of the Elizabethan system of government in her latter years to suggest that her reputation as the leader of a united kingdom was only just maintained. This can be studied in the career of the Earl of Essex, who abused the current convention of courtly love by playing on the old Queen's need of affection, built up an alternative system of government, bullied the Queen into appointing him to military commands and then attempted a *coup d'etat* in 1601.

In the same year, parliament began questioning the Queen's prerogative, the basis of her authority, in the monopolies debate. It was only her advanced age and what became known as her Golden Speech that diverted a challenge that was more dangerous to the future of the monarchy than Essex's half-hearted assault on London.

As a political leader, Elizabeth has a reputation for putting off decisions, and this could have undermined the day by day working of the government. In some instances, she appears to have made up her mind and then changed it. She was clever at finding reasons why a decision should not be made or at devising compromises. There were ministers round her who seemed much more ready to make decisions and even to make decisions for her. This leads the historian to wonder whether the Queen was really in charge or was delaying decisions through a stubborn intention not to be dominated by males. It is also necessary to look out for occasions when the Queen did make up her mind, and to assess whether or not she was judicious in her decision making.

Similar criteria are involved in considering Elizabeth as a war leader. Here her main role was to devise the strategy, to make the high-level decisions and to choose the commanders. Her caution has sometimes been

'Golden Speech': this was made to the House of Commons in 1601, admitting the Queen's error in distributing monopolies, and frankly seeking to regain their love and affection.

An engraving of Elizabeth by William Rogers. Elizabeth carries the orb and sceptre, the symbols of power. The Queen is shown looking older, but still wears similar decorative clothes.

shown in a disadvantageous light, in comparison with the heroic individualistic exploits of her subjects. Still, she did guide the country through a dangerous phase of its history, although it is worth asking how much her success owed to circumstances and how much to good judgement. Some would say that had she sought to influence events more forcefully, the war might have been shorter. On the other hand, an unglamorous, inexpensive and safe strategy had obvious advantages for a relatively weak power such as England. On this and other issues, final judgement will depend on establishing whether Elizabeth identified England's vital interests, and on assessing how well she defended them.

The Background

Europe Divided: Conspiracy and Religious Conflict

Elizabeth was the child of Henry VIII and Anne Boleyn, and was conceived out of wedlock. The couple waited a long time for the Pope to grant Henry VIII a divorce from his wife, Catherine of Aragon, and when it became clear that the Pope would not do so, Henry took matters into his own hands, having her first marriage declared null and hurriedly marrying Anne. Henry was convinced that the inability of his first wife, Catherine of Aragon, to give him a boy-child was divine punishment for a sacrilegious marriage. Catherine of Aragon had been previously married to his brother, Arthur, and there was a passage in the Bible which said, 'And if a man shall take his brother's wife, it is an unclean thing, he hath uncovered his brother's nakedness; they shall be childless' (Leviticus 20.21). Catherine had produced a number of children, but only one, Mary, had survived.

The Pope's refusal to sanction Henry's divorce led the King to break with the Roman Catholic Church; the Church of England became an independent institution with the monarch at its head. Henry was disappointed that Anne Boleyn's child, born on 7 September 1533, was a girl, the later Queen Elizabeth. The circumstances of her birth ensured that she would be associated with the anti-papal movement in England.

Henry VIII's break with the Pope did not leave England isolated in Europe, since there was already a widespread revolt against Rome on

Henry VIII's family. Henry VIII is seated with his arm round his son Edward, later Edward VI (1547-1553). His last wife Catherine Parr sits next to him. Standing on the left and right are Mary, later Mary I (1553-1558) and Elizabeth, later Elizabeth I (1558-1603).

purely religious grounds. This was Protestantism, which began as a movement against undoubted abuses within the Church, and developed into a separate 'Reformed Religion', bitterly hostile to Catholicism and differing from it on many points of belief and practice. Although he had thrown off the Pope's authority, Henry VIII was not a Protestant; but he followed the Protestants' example in dissolving monasteries and chantries, and taking over their property. Since much of this property was later sold off to the English nobility and gentry, a large section of the ruling class acquired a material interest in the new anti-papal order; and it was likely that, in the right circumstances, they would be attracted to the Reformed Religion.

Henry VIII subsequently married four more times, but it was the third wife, Jane Seymour, who produced the son, Edward, whom he desired. This completed Henry's family of two girls and a boy, all of whom survived to rule England.

As the male, Edward succeeded his father as Edward VI (1547-1553). During his reign the Church in England became a Protestant Church with its own Prayer Book, setting out all the services in English (instead of in Latin, as in the Roman Catholic Church). Edward's older sister, Mary, ruled from 1553 to 1558. As Catherine of Aragon's daughter, she was committed to Catholicism; she reversed most of the changes in the Church that Henry VIII and Edward VI had made, although the monastic and chantry lands were not restored. England was received back into the bosom of the Roman Catholic Church, the Latin services were resumed, and Protestant bishops were replaced by Catholics.

Mary I and Philip II. Mary I, or Mary Tudor as she is also known, brought great unpopularity on herself by marrying Philip of Spain in 1554. Philip became ruler of Spain as Philip II in 1556 and lived until 1598. It was Philip II who dispatched the Armada against England in 1588.

Thomas Cranmer (1486-1556) was Archbishop of Canterbury from 1533 until Mary's reign, when he was imprisoned and then burned for heresy in 1556. He drafted the two versions of the Prayer Book in 1549 and 1552.

Thomas Cromwell (1485?-1540) was chief adviser to Henry VIII from 1532 to 1540, when he was executed. He was responsible for much government reform, including the reorganization of the Privy Council and the formation of the Welsh counties.

Mary became associated in people's minds with domination by a foreign Catholic power because she chose to marry the man who became King of Spain as Philip II. Englishmen feared that their interests would be subordinated to Spain's, and that the Spaniards might gain too much influence in England. Mary also lost popularity because she persecuted 'heretics' so ferociously: during her four-year reign, 300 Protestants were burnt in Smithfield, and at Oxford, three Protestant bishops, including the Archbishop of Canterbury, Thomas Cranmer, went to the stake.

Mary's reign ended in gloom, and much was expected of Elizabeth when she came to the throne at the age of 25. She inherited a war with France that had proved very unpopular as it had resulted in the loss of Calais, England's last possession on the continent. Scotland was under French control, ruled as it was by the French regent, Mary of Guise. The young Queen, Mary Queen of Scots, was married to the heir to the King of France; she was sixteen in 1558 and had an excellent claim to the English throne. The French therefore posed a real danger to the new Queen.

The general position of England in 1558 gave Elizabeth some disadvantages and some advantages. Among the disadvantages were the rise in prices that had occurred in the previous ten years. The crown was not able to take advantage of rising prices as it tried to set a good example by keeping the rents on crown lands as steady as possible. The real return from crown lands therefore tended to go down.

Two obvious ways of raising quick money, by selling land or by tampering with the coinage, had already been tried by Elizabeth's predecessors, with negative results. There were dangers in expecting to raise large sums of money through parliament, as parliament might try to tell the Queen how she should spend it. Elizabeth therefore accepted that the crown was becoming poorer and tried to keep down the cost of government.

On the other hand, Elizabeth had much to be thankful for in the area of political and financial administration. Thomas Cromwell had been responsible for a major reform of government in the reign of Henry VIII and this improved royal control over the system of government. The Queen used a small Privy Council of carefully chosen councillors on the model devised by Thomas Cromwell. She also inherited royal councils in Wales and the North, which improved royal control over the outlying areas of her kingdom. Financial courts established by Thomas Cromwell had been reformed and adapted under the direction of the long-serving Lord Treasurer, the Marquis of Winchester, who remained in office when Elizabeth came to the throne.

Most local government remained in the hands of unpaid local worthies called justices of the peace (JPs), whose responsibilities were increased. These worthies were chosen from among the wealthy non-noble landowners who had benefited from the sale of crown land and the rise of prices; as a class they are known as the gentry. The gentry were becoming better educated and therefore more willing to take part in public affairs; many studied at Oxford or Cambridge or one of the Inns of Court, acquiring a grounding in the law. They came to see the House of Commons as a medium through which they could make known their views. Control of parliament by the crown therefore became increasingly difficult. The House of Commons was capable of being a powerful ally, an irritating critic or a potential rival. Elizabeth was forced to exercise great skill to keep it under her control.

In foreign affairs, France was England's traditional enemy, but during Elizabeth's reign, fear of France was lessened through the successful

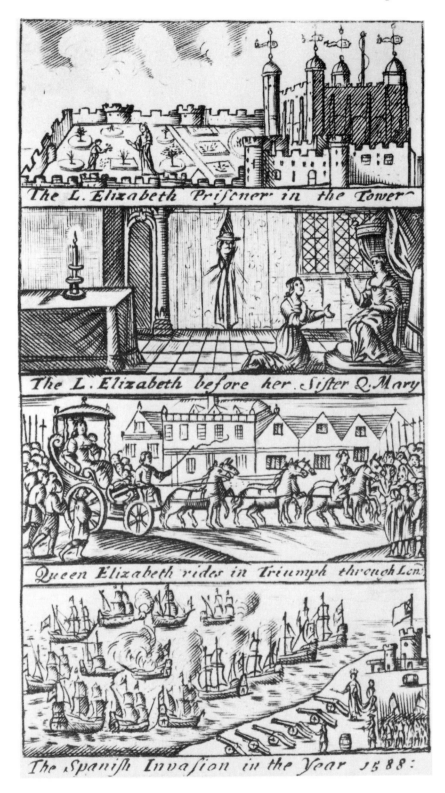

The L. Elizabeth Prisoner in the Tower.

The L. Elizabeth before her Sister Q. Mary

Queen Elizabeth rides in Triumph through Lon.

The Spanish Invasion in the Year 1588:

Episodes in the life of Elizabeth. She was put in the Tower in the time of the Wyatt rebellion 1554 and had to plead her innocence before her sister, Mary Tudor. After a period in which her fate seemed uncertain, she was sent to Woodstock in Oxfordshire under the care of Sir Henry Bedingfield.

removal of the French army from Scotland by the 1560 Treaty of Edinburgh and by the weakness caused by the French wars of religion.

Spain had become even more powerful than France during the sixteenth century. Philip II possessed an enormous empire, and precious metals from Mexico and Peru gave him an accessible source of new wealth. England valued the Spanish alliance, but sources of friction increased. English

William Paulet, Marquis of Winchester (1485-1572). He brought experience to Elizabeth's government as he had been Lord Treasurer to Edward VI and to Mary Tudor. He remained Lord Treasurer until his death in 1572, when Lord Burghley took over. Asked how he weathered the revolutions of four reigns, he said, 'Why, I am sprung from the willow and not from the oak.'

pirates and interlopers trespassed on the Spaniards' American colonies. The Spanish army in the Netherlands, which arrived in 1567, was felt to be uncomfortably close to the shores of England. In addition to this, Philip II was tempted to befriend the English Catholics in plots against Elizabeth. By 1585, Spain had become a real enemy, representing an alien Catholic ideology and posing a real threat to the English state.

The weakness that Spain could exploit was the existence of a Catholic minority of uncertain size. England did not become an exclusively Protestant country in 1559 when Elizabeth's first Parliament imposed a Protestant settlement on England. English Catholics could hope that a change of ruler could lead to the restoration of a Catholic Church. If Elizabeth were to die, her successor would be Mary Queen of Scots, a Catholic.

This situation became even more critical in 1568, when events brought Mary herself to England. Having been widowed as Queen of France, Mary had become the resident ruler of Scotland and had proceeded to fall out with her Protestant noblemen. She had made a disastrous marriage with Lord Darnley in 1565 and was widely believed to have been implicated in his murder in 1567 at Kirk o' Fields. She had then married Lord Bothwell in doubtful circumstances and had been deprived of her throne before escaping to England. This presented Elizabeth with a most difficult problem and she has been criticized on moral grounds for her decision to keep Mary as a perpetual prisoner who had been found neither innocent nor guilty of any crime. From a political point of view the disadvantage of this decision was that Mary remained as a magnet for Catholic plotters.

A particularly dangerous episode was the Rebellion of the Northern Earls (1569), which started as a court intrigue and ended as a feudal rebellion led by the northern lords. The co-ordination of the Catholic effort was awry, as the Pope did not announce Elizabeth's excommunication from the Catholic Church until the rebellion was over. The excommunication of Elizabeth in 1570 was very important as it declared

Mary Queen of Scots (1542-1587). At the beginning of Elizabeth's reign, Mary was Queen of Scotland, married to the King of France's heir and had the best claim to the English throne should Elizabeth die. Her presence as a captive in England (1568-87) constituted one of the major problems of Elizabeth's reign.

that Elizabeth should be dethroned and required English Catholics to withdraw their allegiance from her.

During the following years there were a number of plots to kill Elizabeth, which involved the Spanish ambassadors and the Guise family in France, the most important being the Ridolfi Plot (1571), the Throckmorton Plot (1583) and the Babington Plot (1586). After 1575, Catholic missionaries began to arrive in England to reconvert the country. The government treated them savagely, claiming that they were hunted down and executed as traitors, not for their religious convictions; whether the distinction is a meaningful one remains a matter of opinion.

Elizabeth was far more patient in the face of these threats than her ministers, but by 1587 she had been persuaded that Mary Queen of Scots should be executed for her part in the Babington Plot. By that time, England was at war with Spain and had an army in the Netherlands trying to stop the Duke of Parma from gaining a victory over the Protestant rebels of the Northern Provinces of Holland and Zeeland.

The Spanish Armada had been ready to embark on the 'Great Enterprise' of invading England in 1587, but the Spanish fleet waiting in Cadiz harbour was destroyed by an expedition led by Sir Francis Drake. The Armada sailed in 1588 and progressed up the English Channel tracked by the English galleons. The Spanish had no deep water port on the

Mary Queen of Scots and Lord Darnley married in July 1565. Both had a claim to the English throne. The marriage was a great encouragement to Catholics as they hoped that they would have Catholic children to secure a Catholic future for Scotland and England. The marriage was a great threat to the Congregation of Scottish nobles like the Earl of Murray and there was some satisfaction when the marriage began to fail.

Netherlands coast and had to anchor in open sea. English fire ships were able to dislodge them, after which the English fleet defeated them at Gravelines. The Spaniards fled north, sailing right round the British Isles to get back to Spain and suffering even more cruelly from the Atlantic gales than from the attentions of the English fleet.

The defeat of the Armada did not end the Spanish threat, and new Armadas were prepared, only to be scattered by unfavourable weather. Elizabeth has been criticized for not blockading the Spanish navy more effectively. This was particularly the case in the Portugal expedition of 1589 which identified the right target, the Armada ships in the north Spanish ports, but was lured to the alternative targets of Lisbon and the Azores by the temptation of better profits. Elizabeth also sent armies to Normandy and Brittany in the period 1590-1595, but only to indicate to her ally Henry IV of France her interest in keeping the adjacent French ports out of Spanish hands. During this period, one after another of Elizabeth's trusted ministers and courtiers died – Leicester in 1588, Walsingham in 1590, and William Cecil, Lord Burghley, in 1598. There was a struggle at court between a 'total war' party led by Robert Devereux, Earl of Essex, and the

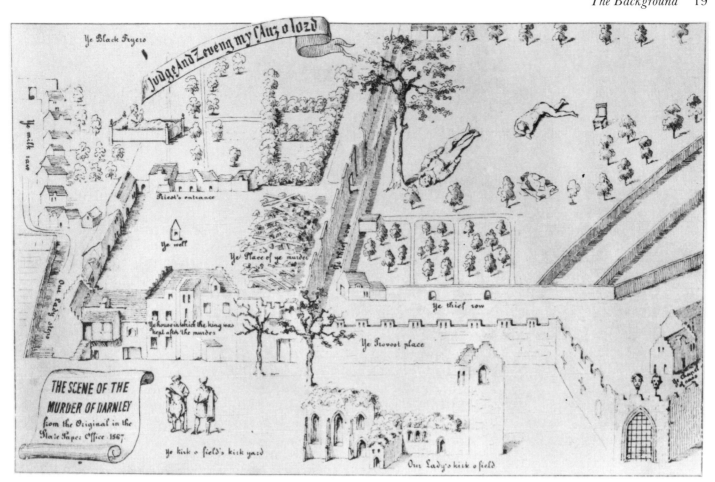

Within the illustration, the following labels appear:

Ye Black Fryers · Judge And Zeveng my (Auz o lozd · Ye mill raw · Priest's entrance · Ye well · Ye Place of ye murder · Ye thief row · Ye house in which the king was kept after the murder · Our Lady's steps · Ye Provost place · THE SCENE OF THE MURDER OF DARNLEY from the Original in the State Paper Office 1567 · Ye kirk o' field's kirk yard · Our Lady's kirk o' field

Lord Darnley was found murdered in 1567 at Kirk o' Fields. The house was blown up, but his half-naked body was found in the grounds. Mary Queen of Scots was accused of complicity, and her failure to mount a thorough investigation of the crime made the accusation seem plausible. She was subsequently deprived of her throne and escaped to England in 1568. Elizabeth found the case against Mary Queen of Scots not proved but held her a prisoner.

cautious party led by Robert Cecil, Lord Burghley's son. Resources were frittered away by Essex in a very successful, but indecisive raid on Cadiz in 1596 and a fruitless attempt to capture the Spanish treasure fleet in 1597. Essex then lost his reputation during his command of the Queen's army in Ireland in 1599. His challenge to the Queen's authority in his abortive rebellion in 1601 revealed the shortcomings of Elizabeth's trust in favourites, but when the reign ended the wise but careful Cecil was still in control. One of the Queen's last acts was to whisper the name of James VI of Scotland as her successor. The issue of the succession which had been most important to her subjects was the last one to be resolved.

Interpretations

The Young Elizabeth. This is a picture of Elizabeth aged about 13. She was an excellent scholar. It was said by her tutor Robert Ascham, 'Yea, I believe that beside her perfact readiness in Latin, French and Spanish, she readeth here now at Windsor more Greek every day, than some prebendary of this Church does read Latin in a week.'

A Virgin Queen

Elizabeth must have been very conscious that the future of England depended on her own life. Had she died from smallpox in 1562 – and she nearly did – Mary Queen of Scots might well have succeeded, though not without a challenge from a Protestant claimant such as Lady Catherine Grey. Civil war would have been a distinct possibility. Yet Elizabeth would not necessarily have solved the problem by marrying and having a child, as the child at that point would have been too young to stop faction-fighting (though at least an undisputed heir). The outlook beyond Elizabeth was bleak and a worry to her Council and her Parliament.

Elizabeth approached marriage in a calculating manner and must have seen it in terms of gains and losses. Parliament wanted her to marry an Englishman, but historical precedents for an English monarch marrying a subject were not encouraging, except for Henry VII's marriage to Elizabeth of York. Edward IV created considerable trouble for himself by his love-marriage to Elizabeth Woodville; and Henry VIII's marriages to his subjects had contributed to faction-fighting. Marriage to a foreign king or prince had been discredited by the immense unpopularity of Mary Tudor's marriage to Philip II of Spain.

Elizabeth seems to have calculated that her virginity would be seen as a positive asset. She could attract the loyalty of her courtiers by holding out the hope of marriage, without ever giving more than the fruits of royal favour, such as land or monopolies. In return she expected them to behave like suitors. She was less disturbed by their sexual indiscretions than by their marriage to someone else. Leicester tried to keep his marriage to Lettice Knollys a secret in 1578 and Raleigh was imprisoned in the Tower and lost favour for five years for giving a maid of honour a child and then, more unpardonably, marrying her. The Queen's eligibility would also be a continuing asset in the diplomatic field as the great powers could always hope to win England by a marriage.

She also may have understood the usefulness of the reputation of a Virgin Queen. She always emphasized her devotion to her realm and people, and marriage to her job emphasized this dedication. She would not have liked to be called the mother of her people, but she did cherish the image of a semi-divine maiden princess, especially during the later years of her reign.

Elizabeth and Leicester

When Elizabeth came to the throne she was 25 and it is surprising that she had not married already. Her early life had been blighted by being for a time legally judged a bastard and she had been fostered out in her teens. In her sister's reign the Wyatt rebels had wanted her to marry a Protestant as part of their campaign against Mary Tudor's Spanish marriage. She may well have been put off marriage and really did intend to live and die a virgin. It may have been another aspect of her indecision. The Spanish

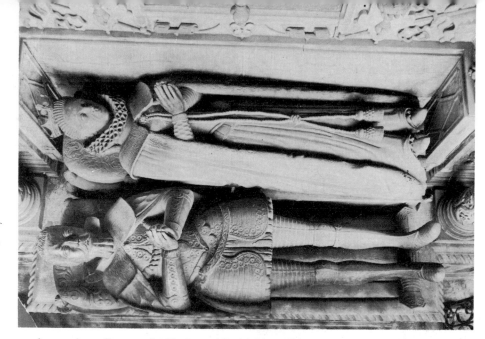

The tomb of Robert Dudley, Earl of Leicester, and his second wife, Lettice Knollys, in the church of St Mary, Warwick. Robert Dudley was Elizabeth's favourite and a trusted councillor in the first part of the Queen's reign. He always regarded William Cecil as a rival.

ambassador, Count de Feria said, 'After all, everything depends on the husband she chooses', and he may have been right.

The calculated nature of Elizabeth's indecision still baffles all commentators. There is every reason to believe that she was capable of love, judging by the rumours flying round at the beginning of the reign of her love for Robert Dudley, Earl of Leicester. The fact that he was already married and that his wife Amy Robsart mysteriously died by falling down the stairs at Cumnor Place, near Oxford, in 1560, always made for rather scandalous gossip – and made marriage to Leicester out of the question, raising the possibility that Amy had been murdered in order to get her out of the way.

Elizabeth's intention to remain a virgin:

For although I be never so careful of your well doings and mind ever so to be, yet may my issue grow out of kind and become perhaps ungracious. And in the end, this shall be for me sufficient, that a marble stone shall declare that a Queen, having reigned such a time, lived and died a virgin.
Quoted in J.E. Neale, *Elizabeth and her Parliaments 1559-1581*, Cape 1953

Rumour of her love for the Earl of Leicester:

On St George's Day, 23 April 1559, the patron saint of the Knights of the Garter, she attended the ceremony then performed, never having attended it before. With the consent of the chapter, the Queen created the Earl of Arundel her Vicegerent and three knights, the Duke of Norfolk, the Earl of Rutland and Lord Robert Dudley, Master of the Horse and son of the late Duke of Northumberland, a very handsome young man, towards whom in various ways the Queen evinces such affection and inclination that many persons believe that if his wife, who has been ailing for some time, were perchance to die, the Queen might easily take him for her husband.
From *Calendar of State Papers Venetian 1558-1580* (edited by Rawdon Brown) 1890.

Marriage Plans

Parliament, aided and abetted by the Council, put great pressure on Elizabeth to marry. Elizabeth never allowed them to bully her, but she did engage in some serious negotiations to marry foreign princes. The main suspicion of foreign courts was that there was something wrong with Elizabeth and that she was incapable of bearing children. The difficulty from Elizabeth's point of view was that the most eligible candidates were Catholics, who wanted to continue their Catholic worship once they came

Elizabeth said this in her first speech to Parliament in 1559. Elizabeth always spoke elegantly, but never plainly. This is likely to have been said for effect, for just before she had talked about 'God inclining her to another kind of life,' and 'whomsoever my chance shall be to light upon,' which seem to imply that she might have been considering marriage.

Vicegerent: a deputy.

Venice was a leading Italian city republic and the Venetian ambassadors were great news gatherers. Does this report lead you to think that Amy Robsart's death was not an accident?

This is a miniature of Elizabeth by Nicholas Hilliard. Hilliard was the Queen's official miniaturist and he was allowed to go to France in the service of Anjou 1576-1578.

to live in England. In the earlier part of her reign she considered marriage to Archduke Charles, the son of the Holy Roman Emperor, though she never displayed much enthusiasm. After the signing of a treaty with France in 1572, she became interested in marrying a brother of the French King. She seems to have been more emotionally involved in the courtship of the Duke of Anjou than with any other suitor, and there is a suspicion that by 1579 desperation was creeping in. She was then 46, and her councillors thought that she was too old for childbirth. Some of her subjects opposed the idea of a Catholic marriage. The Queen seemed genuinely sorry when she felt compelled to withdraw from the marriage plans and this sorrow is reflected in her poems written at the time (page 24). It must also be remembered that Elizabeth needed to keep her eye on the Duke of Anjou, as he was helping William the Silent and the Northern Provinces in their fight against Spain in the Netherlands. Perhaps the political and diplomatic consideration was uppermost in this case too.

Elizabeth's fertility:

The Queen's physician said this to the French ambassador in 1566 when the French King, Charles IX, was considering a marriage to Elizabeth.

If the King marries her, I guarantee ten children; and no one in the world knows her constitution better than I do.
Quoted in J.E. Neale, *Queen Elizabeth I.*

Elizabeth said this to a delegation from both Houses of Parliament who wanted to know her intentions regarding marriage and the succession during the 1566 Parliament. The person that Elizabeth was considering as a husband at this time was Archduke Charles. The fact that France and the Empire were interested in marriage in 1566 suggests that Elizabeth's hand in marriage was an attraction. Can we take her statement at face value, or was Elizabeth just pacifying parliament?

This is a letter addressed to the Queen, written by Sir Philip Sidney, Leicester's nephew, who moved in courtly circles and died in the Netherlands at Zutphen in 1586. Monsieur was the title given to the French King's eldest brother.

This is a passage from John Stubbs's 'The Discovery of a gaping gulf wherein England is like to be swallowed by an other French marriage, if the Lord forbid not the banns by letting Her Majesty see the sin and punishment thereof.' The description is of Francis, Duke of Anjou, and indicates Stubbs's contempt for Elizabeth's intended husband. Stubbs had his hand chopped off for this offence.

Elizabeth intends to marry:

And therefore I say again, I will marry as soon as I can conveniently, if God take not him away with whom I mind to marry, or myself, or else some other great let happen. I can say no more, except the party were present. And I hope to have children, otherwise I would never marry.

Quoted in J.E. Neale, *Elizabeth I and her Parliaments 1559-1581*.

Sir Philip Sidney opposes the marriage:

As for his man (Anjou), as long as he is but Monsieur in might and a Papist in profession, he neither can nor will greatly stead you. And if he grow king, his defence will be like Ajax's shield, which weighed down rather than defended those that bore it.

Quoted in Kervyn de Lettenhove, *Relations politiques des Pay-Bas et L'Angleterre*, Brussels, 1891.

John Stubbs attacks the marriage:

. . . this odd fellow, by birth a Frenchman, by profession a Papist, an atheist by conversation, an instrument in France of uncleanness, a fly worker in England for Rome and France in this present affair, a sorcerer by common voice and fame.

Quoted in Wallace MacCaffrey, *Queen Elizabeth and the Making of Policy 1572-1588*, Princeton, 1981.

The Queen's Council opposes the marriage:

What the Council reported to her (the Queen) was not an outright rejection but a stalling motion, i.e. that they could only report the pro and con arguments without coming down on either side. The Queen was indignant, fell to tears and declared she should never have put the question to discussion. In a second interview she reproved those who opposed the match, made light of their fears of Anjou's Catholicism, and expressed astonishment that there should be any doubt of the

Francis, Duke of Anjou (1554-1584). Elizabeth suggested that she should marry this younger man in 1579. At this time, Anjou had undertaken to give military help to William the Silent in the Netherlands. There is every reason to believe that Elizabeth wanted the match made, but that her councillors did not.

This emotional reaction from Elizabeth to the Council's decision not to support the marriage is used as evidence of her romantic interest in the match. It is also significant that the Queen would not go against the Council's recommendation.

advantages of the match; indeed she thought there would have been a universal request that she proceed.

Quoted in Wallace MacCaffrey, *Queen Elizabeth and the Making of Policy 1572-1588.*

The Queen writes poems about her conflicting thoughts on marriage:

When I was fair and young and favour graced me
Of many was I sought, their Mistress for to be:
But I did scorn them all and answered them therefore
Go, go, go, seek some other where
Importune me no more.

These are verses from two separate poems written by Elizabeth. The second is associated with the wooing of Anjou, though it is attributed to a subsequent visit of Anjou in 1581. Both indicate a battle within Elizabeth's heart. The first is earlier and suggests an unwillingness to allow her heart to influence her rational decision to remain unmarried. The second seems to show that she was hiding her true feelings.

I grieve and dare not show my discontent!
I love, and yet am forced to seem to hate!
I do, yet dare not say, I never meant!
I seem stark mute, but inwardly do prate!
I am, and not; I freeze, and yet am burned
Since from myself my other self I turned.

N.L. Frazer, *English History in Contemporary Poetry No. 111*, Historical Association, 1970.

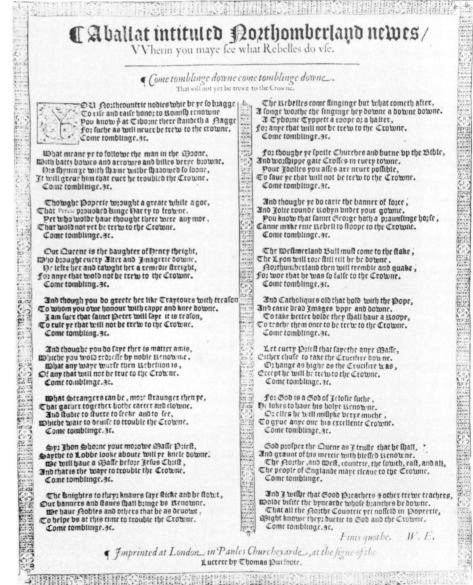

A ballad about the Rebellion of the Northern Earls (1569). The ballad attacks rebels and Catholics. Its main aim is to encourage allegiance to the crown, but there are many references to Catholic practices – the Mass, images, crucifixes etc.

The Possibility of Civil War

There was always a danger in Elizabeth's reign that a substantial faction would declare for Mary Queen of Scots as Elizabeth's most likely successor. The civil war that this might cause would not necessarily be the result of fear about the succession. It could also be caused by noblemen who thought that they had something to gain. This mixture of possibilities was involved in the Rebellion of the Northern Earls in 1569. There was a direct connection between the activities of her councillors and their fear for the succession. Mary Queen of Scots was then a prisoner in England and some felt that she could best be controlled by marriage. A group of councillors thought that William Cecil should be replaced for endangering England's alliance with Spain. In addition there were nobles in the north who were anxious for an excuse to restore the Catholic Church in England.

All these plots came to the Queen's notice in September 1569, when Leicester confessed his part in them. The Duke of Norfolk, whose marriage to Mary Queen of Scots was being planned, came to London and was imprisoned. The Earls of Northumberland and Westmorland refused their invitation to come to London and instead called their tenants to Durham and celebrated Mass there in November 1569. The rebels then marched south as far as Bramham Moor to the west of York, before returning northwards and fleeing into Scotland. The north was punished for its disloyalty both by the dispoilment of the countryside and by the execution of many poor people.

This rebellion casts doubt on the wisdom of Elizabeth over the succession question, her treatment of Mary Queen of Scots, and her control of her own Council. The severity of the punishment of the north was recognition of how dangerous this rebellion was, but it says nothing for Elizabeth's reputation for moderation and mercy.

The reasons for the Duke of Norfolk's marriage plans:

Bruit: a rumour.

At this time a bruit ran amongst men of better note, that the Duke of Norfolk should marry the Queen of Scots, which according to men's affections was upon different reasons desired, while the Papists hoped that hereby their religion would be advanced, and others that it would make for the good of the Commonwealth.

Thomas Howard, Duke of Norfolk (1536-1572), was executed for his implication in plots against Elizabeth. He pleaded his innocence in 1569, but in 1571 he was proved to be implicated in a similar plot, involving his marriage to Mary Queen of Scots, arranged by an Italian banker called Ridolfi.

Certainly very many . . . thought it would make more for the settling of things and the keeping the Queen of Scots within her bounds, 'if she were joined in marriage to the Duke of Norfolk, the greatest and noblest man of all nobility of England, a man of great favour with the people, and bred up in the Protestant religion, than if she were married to a foreign prince.'

Amongst these consulters were the Earls of Arundel, Northumberland, Westmorland, Sussex, Pembroke and Southampton, with many Barons, yea and Leicester also himself. All which notwithstanding were of opinion, that the matter was first to be imparted to the Queen, and left to her will and pleasure.

Soon after the rumour of this marriage came more clearly to Queen Elizabeth's ears, by means of the women of the Court, who do quickly smell out love-matters . . . the Queen took the Duke to her Board at Farnham and pleasantly gave him warning 'to beware upon what pillow he leaned his head'.
William Camden, *Annals of Queen Elizabeth 1615*, London 1635.

> **The Norfolk – Mary Queen of Scots marriage consultations concerned a wide cross-section of the nobility and were obviously a matter of great concern to the Queen.**

Norfolk denies his part:

What! Should I seek to marry her, being so wicked a woman, such a notorious adulteress and murderer? I love to sleep upon a safe pillow. I count myself, by your Majesty's favour, as good a prince at home in my bowling-alley at Norwich, as she is, though she were in the midst of Scotland. And if I should go about to marry her, knowing as I do, that she pretendeth a title to the present possession of your Majesty's crown, your Majesty might justly charge me with seeking your own crown from your head.
Quoted in J.E. Neale, *Queen Elizabeth I*.

> **Thomas, Duke of Norfolk said this to the Queen in 1569. The Duke was put in prison until 1570, but was implicated in treason and executed in 1572. The 'wicked woman' is Mary Queen of Scots, who is alleged to have murdered her husband Lord Darnley and to have committed adultery with Lord Bothwell.**

The Earl of Northumberland tells why he rebelled:

When did you first enter this conspiracy? Answer: We first began to talk of these matters when the Duke went in displeasure from Court to his house in London and it was bruited in Yorkshire that the Council was wonderfully divided about the succession, that the Duke and other noblemen had retired to their houses and that the realm would be in a hurly-burly; so I sent to the Duke and assembled my friends, to know their inclinations. I and many gentlemen intended to join the Duke, if the quarrel were for reformation of religion or naming a successor, but not to hazard myself for the marriage.
Quoted in Anthony Fletcher, *Tudor Rebellions*, Longmans, 1968.

> **Answers given by the Earl of Northumberland to questions asked by Lord Hunsdon in 1572. The Duke in this passage is the Duke of Norfolk. The Earl of Northumberland makes it quite clear that he was not interested in supporting Norfolk's marriage to Mary Queen of Scots, but that he was concerned with religion and the succession. What part did rumour play in all this trouble?**

This picture illustrates the Rebellion of the Northern Earls (1569) and the fate of the Earl of Northumberland in 1572. Elizabeth took cruel vengeance on the feudal tenantry who had followed their lords. The work of punishing and pacifying the North was carried out by a commission which included Lord Hunsdon, the governor of Berwick.

Elizabeth as a religious leader

Elizabeth's accession was received with great enthusiasm by the City of London in November 1558. It is easy to presume from this that the enthusiasm for Elizabeth as a Protestant successor was country-wide. There is no doubt that areas farther from London were very attached to the old religion and would have been happy to continue in their Catholic worship.

The print illustrates the two extremes which Elizabeth needed to reconcile. To the left Edward VI receives communion according to Protestant rites, with the priest wearing no vestments and kneeling on the north side of the altar. To the right the Oxford martyrs are being burnt in Mary's reign, though Bishop Ridley and Bishop Latimer were not burnt at the same time as Archbishop Cranmer. The favoured Edward VI kneels devoutly at the altar, while Mary looks on with satisfaction from the balcony. Elizabeth presides over it all with a strange cornucopia of flowers.

One shilling = 5p. A considerable sum of money in Elizabeth's reign.

Richard Hooker: leading English Theologian and Reformer.

John Foxe (1516-1587). He was author of the Book of Martyrs, *which celebrated the lives and deaths of all the Protestants who were punished for their faith during the Reformation. He must be counted as one of the founders of the anti-Catholic tradition in England, as his book was extraordinarily popular.*

It is generally agreed that the Church Settlement which Elizabeth guided through Parliament was politically motivated. Her main priority was to heal the religious division that threatened to divide her realm. Her intention was to impose an early settlement which would enable her subjects to express their religious convictions within the structure that she and her Parliament had provided. Church-going was to be an outward expression of loyalty and those who refused to attend would be fined at the rate of one shilling each week. The implication of the Settlement was that the Queen was not too concerned about people's religious opinions as long as they conformed outwardly. There would be a degree of tolerance for dissent.

The main criticism of Elizabeth's policy was that her political priorities stifled the possibility of satisfying the real aspiration of the Reformation, which was to reform the Church. The unpopularity of the Church stemmed from the weakness of the clergy, who were criticized for their privilege, their ignorance, their corruption and their worldliness. The clergy needed to be regenerated. The main hope of revival in the Church on both the Catholic and the Protestant side lay in movements aimed at improving the quality, the education and the spirituality of the clergy. Elizabeth's intention was that, once the Settlement had been made, there should be no further discussion of religious change. When there was doubt in interpreting the Settlement, she preferred the older traditions. It was tradition, as described by Richard Hooker in his *Laws of Ecclesiastical Polity*, that eventually gave the Church of England its distinctive character as a Protestant Church. Hooker was able to describe a Church that had existed in England since the arrival of St Augustine in AD 597 as having a definite tradition of its own.

Meanwhile, two further religious movements had been attacked on the grounds that they were politically dangerous. The Puritan movement sought to reform the Church from within. Puritans wanted the ornaments, vestments and symbols of the Catholic religion removed, but they also wanted to improve the Bible knowledge of clergy and laity. Unfortunately, Puritanism became associated with Presbyterianism, which questioned the whole hierarchy of bishops within the Church and rejected by implication the royal supremacy. From the Catholic side there was a zealous missionary movement that began to infiltrate England in the middle of Elizabeth's reign. Their declared aim was to uphold the faith of the English Catholics, but the English government hunted them down, claiming that they were political agents and traitors, who were seeking to draw Elizabeth's subjects away from their true allegiance.

It is still difficult for those with firmly held religious opinions to remain objective in their judgements of Elizabeth's religious policy. Obviously the political unity which Elizabeth achieved was useful, but was it wise to gain it at the expense of the spiritual development of her own church? Does her treatment of religious opponents really allow the historian to use words like tolerance, moderation or mercy in relation to what she was doing or in what she was attempting to achieve?

The Church Settlement

When Elizabeth came to the throne, England had experienced four years of Catholic rule and a restoration of the Protestant Church was expected. A Protestant Church would receive the support of many of the landed gentry who had purchased former monastic and chantry lands from the crown. They would also have no objection to the resumption of the supremacy over the Church, which Henry VIII had claimed and his daughter Mary had disowned. The most advanced Protestant service book available was the

Prayer Book of 1552 and, even though it had only been used for one year in England, it had been used by the exiled Protestants in Frankfurt during Mary's reign.

It is now generally accepted that Elizabeth devised the Settlement that was guided through parliament in 1559, despite the adamant opposition of the bishops from Mary's reign who remained in office. Elizabeth's aims were so political that there has been some questioning of her religious faith. Shrewdness would have told Elizabeth that faith for a monarch should be a private matter. She must have judged that her sister's strongly expressed religious conviction had worked to her detriment by arousing opposition, such as that expressed in the Wyatt rebellion of 1554.

Detriment: disadvantage.

The settlement was hardly a religious compromise, as it started from the most extreme Protestant position that the Church in England had reached, but Elizabeth did make concessions to Catholic opinion. Most of her subjects were familiar with the Catholic mode of worship and it suggests that Elizabeth did have some feel for popular opinion.

The hope of a new beginning:

This gives a good idea of the hope raised by Elizabeth's accession in 1558. Mary's reign had been a time of bad weather and illness as well as persecution. There was a widespread desire for a new start.

After all the storms, tempestuous and blustering windie weather of queen Marie was overblowne, the darksome clouds of discomfort dispersed; the palpable fogs and mists of most intolerable miserie consumed, the dashing showers of persecution overpast, it pleaseth God to send England a calme quiet season, a cleare and lovely sunshine . . . and a world of blessings by Queen Elizabeth.
Raphael Holinshed, *Chronicles of England, Scotland and Ireland*, 1587, Vol. 4.

Elizabeth's religious life:

William Camden (1551-1623) lived through Elizabeth's reign and had access to much original material. The book was published in Latin in 1615. This passage suggests that Elizabeth engaged in her religious observance seriously, choosing to follow the old ways when she could declare a preference.

Yet was she truly religious, who every day, as soon as she arose, spent some time in prayers to God and afterwards also at set times in her private chapel; every Sunday and Holy day she went into her chapel; neither was there ever any other prince present at God's service with greater devotion. The sermons in Lent attentively she heard being all in black, after the manner of old although she many times said that she had rather talk with God devoutly by prayer than hear others speak eloquently of God.
William Camden, *Annals of Queen Elizabeth 1615*

A modern historian doubts Elizabeth's faith:

Do you see any difference in views between Camden and Elton?

The least known factor is her faith. Perhaps – as we are now commonly told, usually by way of commendation – she had none; certainly she had no patience

Matthew Parker (1504-1575), Archbishop of Canterbury from 1559 to 1575. He revised the articles of religion in 1562 with the assent of convocation, reducing them from 42 to 39. He married, contrary to Catholic ruling and to the disapproval of Elizabeth. While leave-taking from Lambeth Palace, Elizabeth said to Parker's wife, 'Madam , I may not call you; mistress I am ashamed to call you, so I know not what to call you; but I thank you.'

Words spoken by the priest in the Book of Common Prayer 1559, when delivering the bread in the Communion Service. The first statement comes from the 1549 Prayer Book and would have been acceptable to Catholics who adore the host (bread) as the Body of Christ. The second comes from the 1552 Prayer Book and would have been acceptable to Protestants who believe that the taking of the bread is a memorial of the Last Supper and an act of thanksgiving. This was a central issue of the Reformation and the Prayer Book found a compromise that it was hoped would satisfy as many people as possible.

Schism and heresy in this passage refer to Protestantism. Why should weavers and cobblers be more likely to be Protestant? Why are farmers, shepherds and those living in country districts more likely to be Catholic? If only one in a hundred were Protestants, how could Elizabeth believe that Protestantism would unite the nation?

with the quarrels of doctrine and wished to keep the peace. She would not, as she said, put windows into men's souls.

G.R. Elton. *England under the Tudors*, Methuen, 1965

Compromise at the centre of the prayer book:

The Body of our Lord Jesus Christ which was given for thee, preserve thy body and soul unto everlasting life: Take and eat this in remembrance that Christ died for thee, and feed on him in thy heart by faith with thanksgiving.

Book of Common Prayer, Service of Holy Communion

An assessment of Catholic support:

While the common people consist of farmers, shepherds and artisans, the farmers and shepherds are Catholics, nor are any of the artisans infected by schism except those engaged in sedentary crafts, weavers for example, and cobblers, and some of the idlers round court. Again, the most distant parts of the Kingdom are most averse to heresy, Wales for example, and Devon, Westmorland, Cumberland and Northumberland. Since cities are few in England, and small, and since heresy does not live in country districts and scarcely at all in the distant cities, it is the firm judgement of those in a position to know, that not so many as one in a hundred of the English are infected . . . .

A Judgement made by Nicholas Sander, Professor of Canon Law Oxford University in 1561, *Catholic Record Society, Miscellanea 1*, 1905.

Elizabeth and her Bishops

Once the Church Settlement was made, Elizabeth expected her bishops to make sure that the new form of worship was used. This was a very difficult task when the nature of church patronage is considered. Much church patronage was in the hands of lay people who had acquired control of parishes when the monastic properties were put up for sale. Patrons had the valuable right to collect tithes – a tenth of agricultural production in the village – for the support of the parish church and its ministry. Patrons were inclined to collect the tithes and to appoint an ill-educated vicar on a small stipend or salary. Well-educated clergy might hold a number of parishes to support themselves and their families, appointing ill-paid curates to run the churches. As it was difficult for bishops to control clergy appointments, it was even more difficult for them to improve the quality of their ministry.

From one point of view the Church was now under lay control and it was important that the lay Queen gave proper support to her bishops. The evidence seems to indicate that she did not.

One way in which the education of the clergy could be improved was to call them to Bible study and prayer. This is what was involved in the Prophesying movement. The Queen did not like the study groups, because she feared that they might turn into Presbyterian cells and become subversive.

John Whitgift was nicknamed Elizabeth's 'black husband': the blackness is a reference to the colour of the clerical cassock.

The Queen's model Archbishop was John Whitgift, her 'black husband', whose test of priestly worth lay in their subscriptions to three main elements in the Church. Clergy had to subscribe to three articles – to the Queen as Supreme Governor of the Church, to the Prayer Book and to the 39 Articles of Religion. It is interesting that even Lord Burghley found this test rather too inflexible (see quote on page 32).

A way in which Elizabeth weakened the bishops was by forcing them to give up their better land and property in exchange for patronage of churches. This aspect adds fuel to the fire of suspicion that the laity were in an unholy alliance to exploit the Church.

Bishop Cox criticized by Lord North for opposing the Queen's designs on his episcopal estates:

Suffer me, my Lord, I pray you, to put in mind who it is that you deny; it is our dread sovereign lady, our most gracious and bountiful Mistress, who hath abled you even from the meanest estate that may be unto the best bishopric in England. She is our God on earth; if there be perfection in flesh and blood, undoubtedly it is in her Majesty. For she is slow to revenge and ready to forgive. And yet, my Lord, she is right King Henry, her father . . . .
Quoted in Sir Maurice Powicke. *The Reformation in England*, OUP, 1941.

Elizabeth threatens Bishop Cox:

Proud prelate, you know what you were before I made you what you are. If you do not immediately comply with my request, I will unfrock you.
Quoted in A.L. Rowse, *The England of Elizabeth*, Macmillan, 1950.

The value of prophesyings:

Report hath been made to your Majesty concerning these exercises . . . . and these profits and commodities following hath ensued from them.
1. The ministers of the Church are more skilful and ready in Scriptures, and apter to teach their flocks.
2. It withdraweth them from idleness, wandering, gaming etc.
3. Some afore suspected in doctrine are brought hereby to open confession of the truth.
4. Ignorant ministers are driven to study . . . .
5. The opinion of laymen touching the idleness of the clergy is hereby removed.

Lord North wrote this to Richard Cox, Bishop of Ely in 1575. Nobles and gentry had benefited very greatly from the distribution of monastic and church lands. It is tempting to suspect a plot of Queen's gentry to enjoy the estates of the bishops as well. Notice how the Queen is called "our God on earth", and likened to her father, Henry VIII.

This short letter was sent by the Queen to Bishop Cox in 1575 when he refused to give up his London house, Ely Place, in Holborn to the Queen's favourite Sir Christopher Hatton. The Queen also secured Durham House in the Strand for Sir Walter Raleigh in similar fashion. **Prelate**: another word for bishop.

Edmund Grindal, Archbishop of Canterbury, explains the value of prophesyings or exercises to the Queen in December 1576. Their long term effect will be to improve the knowledge and piety of the clergy so that they will earn the respect of the lay people.

Edmund Grindal (1519?-1583), Archbishop of Canterbury from 1575 to 1583. He was suspended from 1577 onwards for his refusal to carry out Elizabeth's order to destroy the Prophesying movement. His original appointment was strongly supported by Lord Burghley.

6. Nothing by experience beateth down popery more than that ministers grow to such good knowledge by means of these exercises that where before there were not three able preachers, now there are thirty meet to preach at St Paul's Cross.
Quoted in G.R. Elton, *The Tudor Constitution.*

Archbishop Grindal refuses to suppress exercises:

Archbishop Grindal wrote to the Queen, giving his refusal to obey her in May 1577. He was suspended from Office until his death in 1583 and the Church was left with no leader to support the Queen as Supreme Governor.

I am forced with all humility and yet plainly, to profess that I cannot with safe conscience and without offence to the majesty of God, give my assent to the suppression of the said exercises; much less can I send out any injunction for the utter and universal subversion of the same.
Quoted in J. Strype, *The History of the Life and Acts of Edmund Grindal*, OUP, 1821.

Lord Burghley, the Queen's Treasurer and chief minister, wrote to John Whitgift, her Archbishop of Canterbury in 1584. Lord Burghley hoped that Puritan clergy would not be forced out of the Church by being asked pointed questions. Puritans, for instance, found it very difficult to swear that the Prayer Book contained nothing contrary to the Word of God. The 'Romish inquisition' refers to the Inquisition in Rome which tried and burnt heretics.

Lord Burghley complains of Archbishop Whitgift's methods:

I know your canonists can defend these (articles of examination) with all perticels, under your Grace's correction, this judicial and canonical sifting of poor ministers is not to edify or reform . . . . Now my good Lord, forbear with my scribbling. I write with testimony of good conscience . . . . I desire concord and unity in the exercise of religion . . . . But I conclude according to my simple judgement, this kind of proceeding is too much savouring of the Romish inquisition, and is rather a device to seek for offenders than to reform any.
Quoted in G.W. Prothero, *Statutes and Constitutional Documents 1558-1625*, OUP, 1894.

Archbishop Whitgift justifies himself:

This is John Whitgift's reply to the last letter. Whitgift thought that the Church that he administered was lacking in discipline and that Burghley was supporting clergy who were 'meanly qualified'. This perhaps was unfair as Whitgift's interrogation of the clergy did force honest, well-educated ministers to tell the truth and as a result, to lose their jobs. It also went against Elizabeth's intention not to put windows into men's souls.

I know your Lordship desireth the peace of the Church, but how is it possible to be procured. After so long liberty and lack of discipline, if a few persons, so meanly qualified as most of them are, should be countenanced against the whole state of the clergy of greatest account for learning, steadiness, wisdom, religion and honesty.
Quoted in G.W. Prothero, *Statutes and Constitutional Documents 1558-1625.*

John Whitgift (1530?-1604), Archbishop of Canterbury from 1583 to 1603. He enjoyed the favour of Elizabeth and vigorously enforced her policy of religious uniformity. He drew up articles aimed at non-conformist ministers in 1583 and obtained increased powers for the high commission court. He was made Privy Councillor in 1586.

The Catholics

It was in 1570 that the Queen's accession day began to be celebrated as a day of rejoicing and thanksgiving. People were asked to rally to the Queen in the face of the Rebellion of the Northern Earls and her excommunication by the Pope. The Papal bull instructed Catholics to withdraw their allegiance from the Queen in obedience to the Pope's ruling that she was no longer a member of the Roman Catholic Church. From this time on, all Catholics were potential traitors and in view of the presence of Mary Queen of Scots in England as a ready-made Catholic leader, the Catholic threat was very real and immediate. Elizabeth's councillors expected Mary Queen of Scots to be executed in 1572, but Elizabeth refrained from such a final solution. Mary remained as Elizabeth's prisoner and was a continual focus of Catholic plots.

The hope that Catholicism would die away in England was shattered by the arrival of young, keen Catholic missionaries, who aimed to keep the Catholic faith in England alive. They began to arrive in 1574 from a college that had been established at Douai in France in 1568 by Cardinal William Allen, and were joined later by the Jesuits from Rome. These missionaries were on the whole harmless, saintly people, but they were treated by the authorities as traitorous servants of the Pope's purposes. Their aim was to enable Catholic believers to continue to attend the Catholic Mass and to persuade them not to conform to Elizabeth's state church. In retaliation, the Queen in Parliament passed an act in 1581 making it a treasonable offence to persuade someone not to attend their parish church, if they were already doing so, which was interpreted as withdrawing a person from their natural obedience to the Queen. It was also treason to be reconciled to the Catholic Church. In addition to this there was a fine of £20 a month for anyone over the age of sixteen who did not attend Church. This was equivalent to a year's income for a moderately wealthy person. There was therefore a vigorous campaign to destroy Catholicism. In fact, 183 Catholic subjects lost their lives for treason between 1577 and 1603. It is against this

William Allen (1532-1594). Cardinal Allen founded the Douai training college for Catholic missionaries in France in 1568 and worked to win back England to Catholicism. Although political discussion was forbidden among his young students, they were prepared for martyrdom. Allen was made a cardinal in 1587 as a signal for the crusade against England. On the eve of the Armada he published an attack on the Queen called 'Admonition to the Nobility and People of England'.

Edmund Campion (1540-1581). Edmund Campion was the most saintly of the Catholic missionaries who suffered martyrdom. This propaganda picture shows him stabbed to the heart and with a halter round his neck. Francis Knollys, a councillor, who was present at the execution, cried out that this was not a case of religion, but of treason; he was evidently afraid that Campion's death would generate sympathy for Catholicism.

background that Elizabeth's moderation, tolerance and mercy have to be judged. If these 183 victims constituted a political danger, then it can still be argued that Elizabeth was tolerant in religion. If, on the other hand, it is felt that some or all were being punished for their religious opinion, then the word 'persecution' becomes more apt.

The Pope's Bull of Excommunication:

The bull was in Latin. This bull was issued by Pope Pius V in 1570. It suggests that Elizabeth's title to the throne was illegal, even though previous Popes, Paul IV and Pius IV, had recognized it.

We do out of the fulness of our Apostolic power declare the aforesaid Elizabeth as being a heretic . . . and to have incurred the sentence of excommunication and to be cut off from the unity of the Body of Christ. And moreover we do declare her to be deprived of her pretended title to the Kingdom aforesaid and of all dominion, dignity and privilege whatsoever . . . . and also the nobility, subjects and people of the said Kingdom and all others who have sworn unto her, to be forever absolved from any oath and all manner of duty, of dominion, allegiance and obedience . . . .
William Camden, *Annals of Queen Elizabeth 1615.*

A view of Catholic conformity:

At the first . . . the greatest part even of those who in their judgements and affections had before been Catholics, did not well discern any great faut, novelty or difference from the former religion . . . in the new sett up by Queen Elizabeth, save only change of language . . . and so easily accommodated themselves thereto.
Quoted in A.H. Dodd, *Life in Elizabethan England*, Batsford, 1961.

Said by a Monmouthshire lawyer who afterwards, as Father Baker, became a devoted Benedictine monk. 'Change of language' refers to the holding of Protestant services in English instead of Latin.

The Jesuit mission attacked in Parliament:

Part of a speech by Sir Walter Mildmay to the 1581 Parliament. The Jesuit mission arrived in England in 1580, led by Robert Parsons. Edmund Campion was another famous member of the group. 'Creeping into the houses' does refer to their normal work, which was to act as chaplains in the great houses of the Catholic gentry who liked to hear Mass.

You see how lately he hath sent hither a sort of hypocrites, naming themselves Jesuits, a rabble of vagrant friars sprung up and coming through the world to trouble the Church of God: whose principal errand is by creeping into the houses and familiarities of men of behaviour and reputation, not only [to] corrupt the realm with false doctrine, but also, under that pretence, to stir sedition.
Quoted in J.E. Neale, *Elizabeth I and her Parliaments 1559-1581.*

This picture shows the punishment of Catholic missionary priests in Elizabeth's reign. They were punished for supposedly adhering to the Papal Bull of Excommunication of 1570, which declared Elizabeth excommunicated and deposed, though Campion didn't deny Elizabeth's right to the throne. The victims were hanged, cut down while still alive, castrated, disembowelled and their internal organs burnt, and their bodies were then cut in pieces.

This was part of Edmund Campion's answer, when asked if there was any reason why sentence should not be passed on him and others, at the end of his trial in 1581 on a charge of conspiring to murder Elizabeth. Campion and two others were hanged, drawn and quartered on 1 December 1581. Campion is referring to the Catholic tradition in England stretching back to St Augustine.

This was part of the testimony of John Rigby, who was put to death for treason in 1600, when the charge under the 1581 Act was that he had ceased to attend church. 'My Princess' refers to the Queen, whom he has always obeyed. What point was served by his death, especially in 1600? The government might have argued that the danger of Spanish invasion was still very real, and a Spanish army did land in Ireland in 1601.

Sir Christopher Hatton's opening oration of the 1589 Parliament recounting the famous victory over the Armada, which is seen as a victory for 'the true religion'. Patriots like Hatton genuinely felt that the Church of England was the only true Church of Christ. Catholics would have felt the opposite and would have put a high priority on the elimination of false religion wherever it was found. The idea of crusades against the Turks was sometimes discussed in this century, but rarely put into practice.

Edmund Campion justifies the Catholic tradition:

The only thing that we have to say is, that if our religion make us traitors, we are worthy to be condemned; but otherwise we have been as good subjects as the queen had. In condemning us you condemn all your own ancestors . . . all that was once the glory of England . . . .
Quoted in Patrick McGrath, *Papists and Puritans under Elizabeth I*, Blandford, 1967

A Catholic lay person defends himself in court:

Secondly, whereas I am charged that I was reconciled from my obedience to her Majesty and to the Romish religion, I will depose the contrary: for I was never reconciled from any obedience to my Princess, for I obey her still; nor to any religion, for although I sometimes went to church against my will, yet was I never of any other religion than the Catholic, and therefore needed no reconciliation to religion.
Quoted in Philip Hughes, *The Reformation in England*, Burn and Oates, 1950.

The Court view of the Spanish Catholic Threat:

Sufficient to show to all posterity the unchristian fury both of the Pope (that wolfish bloodsucker) and of the Spaniard (that insatiable tyrant) in that they never bent themselves with such might and resolution against the very Turk or any other infidel, as they have done against a Virgin Queen, a famous lady, and a country which embraceth without corruption in doctrine the true and sincere religion of Christ.
Quoted in J.E. Neale, *Elizabeth I and her Parliaments 1584-1601*.

Elizabeth as a decision maker

There is no doubt that the Queen governed the country and had responsibility for the most important decisions. Considerations must be

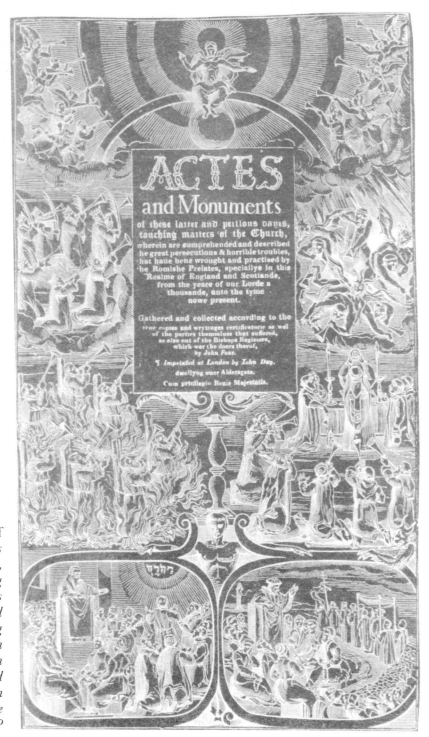

The frontispiece of Foxe's Book of Martyrs *(negative image), which is correctly called* Acts and Monuments, *shows the kingly trumpeters carrying palms and Protestant martyr trumpeters ascending towards heaven on the left, and the fiendish trumpeters of hell descending towards the celebration of the Mass with the host uplifted on the right. At the bottom is Protestant preaching to the left and Catholic preaching with the congregation using rosaries, a procession and a wayside shrine. What is the propaganda message?*

given, however, to the process by which these decisions were made, for, like all rulers, she was supported by ministers and councillors who carried much of the work load. Her father delegated the work of government to trusted ministers like Cardinal Wolsey and Thomas Cromwell, who were responsible for most of the policy and decision making, but were dismissed once they ceased to be useful. Elizabeth also had a chief minister of the kind in William Cecil, Lord Burghley, but he never enjoyed this kind of delegated authority, nor was he ever thrown aside, remaining in high office until his death. Burghley influenced government by seeking to think like the

This is an early official portrait of Elizabeth used for official documents such as this charter granted to Beaumaris in 1561. The ermine cape and ruffs at neck and sleeves emphasize her heart-shaped face. She looks far more ordinary in this portrait than in the later official portraits.

Queen and to see policy through her eyes, so that when she did make decisions, the way for their acceptance and implementation was prepared. It has been suggested, especially by a nineteenth-century historian called Froude, that the achievement in Elizabeth's reign was Lord Burghley's, the loyal, hard-working but self-effacing chief minister, who guided the country despite the Queen's interference.

This emphasis on Burghley diminishes the part played by the Queen's Council which can be described as the nerve-centre of Elizabethan government. Burghley was a member, but he did not dominate it, nor was he able to ignore or bypass it. It was a small but efficient body of trusted people, chosen by the Queen, representing a cross section of opinion within the country. It contained Catholic sympathizers, Puritans, Queen's relations and favourites, and trusted officials. It wasn't always completely loyal, as has been shown by the plan to oust Cecil in 1569, nor was it always united. The Queen rarely attended, so Burghley was the one who usually argued the Queen's case for her. The range of religious views within the Council was reflected in a variety of attitudes to foreign policy, especially in relation to the growing power of Spain. In the 1570s there was a group within the Council with Puritan sympathies, who felt that war with Spain was inevitable and necessary. The main supporters of this view were

William Cecil, Lord Burghley (1520-1598), was Elizabeth's chief minister for most of her reign. The influence of the Cecils was prolonged into the next reign by his son Robert.

Leicester and Walsingham. The irony in Leicester's case was that while he favoured the group seeking to oust William Cecil in 1569, because Cecil was too warlike towards Spain, he then joined the group who opposed Burghley for being too conciliatory. Leicester and Burghley did regard themselves as rivals for the Queen's favour and maybe personal jealousy rather than principle was involved in their disagreement as far as Leicester was concerned.

A number of occasions when the Queen ignored the Council's advice have already been mentioned. There is the case of her refusal to marry, to name her successor, her hesitation in punishing the Duke of Norfolk and Mary Queen of Scots. Further examples will be given of her reluctance to aid foreign rebels and to become involved in foreign war. Her critics put this down to her inability to decide, mainly due to what has been seen as her womanly caution.

What must be examined is whether decisiveness is always a virtue. There are times when decisions have to be taken, but other times when a decision not to decide can be taken. Everyone would condemn dithering, but caution is sometimes sensible. The best decisions are taken after a careful analysis of the situation and the choices. It also helps if there are consistent principles which govern the decision-making, so that individual decisions contribute towards a strategy. Another factor to consider is opportunism. This is the process of delaying a decision until the most advantageous moment, even if this means waiting a long time.

There are some principles of English foreign policy that ought to be borne in mind. The first was that England had natural island defences, which were effective as long as England maintained an adequate navy and naval bases. The second was that Scotland should not be left in the hands of a foreign army. The third was that the coastline on the opposite side of the Channel should not be allowed to fall into the hands of one country.

Elizabeth was a conservative and was happy to do no more in foreign policy than to defend vital interests. She was always short of funds and had to weigh carefully the cost of any action, as did Burghley after 1572, when he became Lord Treasurer. It is fair, therefore, to judge her actions against these basic principles.

There is one last complication in judging Elizabeth's part in decisions; this is the need in diplomacy to mislead the enemy. Elizabeth has been accused by Victorian moralists of lying and this is a valid criticism. Elizabeth would suggest to foreign ambassadors that her ministers were making decisions against her wishes or she would say one thing and do another. This is all part of the general convention of diplomacy and historians have to be conscious of it.

Intervention in Scotland and France 1560-62

Two facts disturbed Englishmen at the beginning of Elizabeth's reign. Mary Tudor had lost Calais to the French, and a French army was occupying Scotland, which was ruled by a French Regent, Mary of Guise. In the scale of English interests, the first fact was unimportant, since Calais was an expensive anachronism, whereas the second seemed very dangerous.

Elizabeth's great early achievement was that the French army had been removed from Scotland by 1560 and Burghley was able to negotiate the terms under which Mary Queen of Scots would rule there. A lasting settlement with Scotland was something that had eluded the previous three rulers and constituted a diplomatic triumph. There is no doubt that luck was involved, but a successful outcome was achieved once the idea of depending on Protestant Scots noblemen had been shelved and an army and navy had been sent. The way in which this decision to intervene was reached throws light on the decision-making process.

The great failure was an attempt in 1562 to help the Protestant movement in France in return for the handing over of the French port of Le Havre, which would then be used as a bargaining counter to win back Calais. The failure of this plan may have been the reason why Elizabeth never liked to base her policy on alliance with foreign Protestant rebels. The real question is: who made the decision to intervene?

Cecil offers his resignation:

With a sorrowful heart and watery eyes, I your poor servant and most lowly subject, an unworthy Secretary, beseech your Majesty to pardon this my lowly suit, that considering the proceeding in this matter for removing the French out of Scotland doth not content your Majesty and that I cannot with my conscience give any contrary advice, I may, with your Majesty's favour and clemency, be spared to entermeddle therein.

Conyers Read, *Mr Secretary Cecil and Queen Elizabeth*, Cape, 1955.

Failure in the siege on Leith:

God trieth us with many difficulties. The Queen's Majesty never liketh this matter of Scotland. . . . And now we looked for best fortune, the worst came. Upon Tuesday the 7th of this month our men offered an assault at Leith and being not saltable they were repulsed with loss of a thousand men. . . . The Queen's Majesty also mindeth the achieving of the matter so earnestly as nothing shall be spared. Order is given to send both men, money and artillery with all possible speed. I have had such a torment herein with the Queen's Majesty, as an ague hath not in five fits so much abated.

Conyers Read, *Mr Secretary Cecil and Queen Elizabeth*.

William Cecil wrote this letter to the Queen in late December 1559. He had persuaded the Council that military intervention in Scotland was necessary and now brought pressure on the Queen by threatening to resign. Resignation was not necessary as the Queen accepted the decision. Cecil's office at this time was Secretary of State. Was the Queen being 'bulldozed' into a decision by her more decisive minister?

Cecil wrote this to Sir Nicholas Throckmorton in May 1560. Cecil's and the Council's advice to intervene seemed questionable in view of this failure. The Queen was clearly not pleased, but did everything she could to redress the situation. The last sentence suggests that the Queen was willing to speak her mind to her ministers.

The Duke of Alva (1508-1582). Alva was the Spanish governor of the Netherlands from 1567 to 1573. The arrival of his army in the Netherlands, and his policy of ruthless repression, marked the end of the period when Spain was England's ally.

Sir Nicholas Throckmorton wrote to Cecil, having heard that he was to be dispatched north to negotiate an end to the Scottish war. He obviously believed that Cecil was indispensable in decision making.

Who else can deal with the Queen but Cecil?

Who can as well stand fast against the Queen's arguments and doubtful devices? Who will speedily resolve the doubtful delays? Who shall make dispatch of anything?
Calendar of State Papers Foreign 1560-1561 (edited by John Stevenson).

Elizabeth prepared to take responsibility:

They say that the Queen was quite furious at the Council, and replied to some of those who opposed the expedition that if they were so much afraid that the consequences of failure would fall upon them, she herself would take all the risk and would sign her name to it.
Calendar of State Papers Spanish 1558-1567 (edited by M. Hume).

The Spanish ambassador De Quadra wrote this to the Duchess of Parma in September 1561. The Queen showed decision here, but it may have been that she was more under the influence of the Earl of Leicester in this phase.

The Netherlands 1577-1578

Elizabeth followed two sound principles in her dealings with the Netherlands that conform to England's traditional interest concerning the coastline on the opposite side of the Channel. The first principle was that she wanted the semi-independence of the Netherlands restored. The second was that she wanted Spain there to stop France expanding northwards into that area. She was not, therefore, going to give her whole and ungrudging support to William the Silent and the Dutch Protestant rebels against Spanish rule.

A Hieroglyphic of Britain from John Dee's Art of Navigation *1577. Elizabeth rides in the ship Christendom, attended by the three estates of the realm and with Europe beside the vessel (Europa and the Bull). The Queen is being entreated by the kneeling Britannia to accept the Victor's crown being offered to her by Occasion. What she needed to do, according to this propaganda picture was to build a navy.*

Some of her councillors at the time, and at least one historian today, believe that Elizabeth was wrong not to give vigorous support to William the Silent in his war against Spain. Spain was on the verge of total defeat in 1576 and it was felt that the Spanish army could have been ejected forever with some timely help to William.

Elizabeth did not want the Spanish presence removed. She was happy that the Spanish were kept busy dealing with the rebellion and she was anxious to keep·an eye on the Duke of Anjou, who represented the French threat and of whom she was equally afraid (see 'Marriage plans', page 22).

Elizabeth criticized for indecision:

The worst damage was inflicted between 1575 and 1579 (and perhaps 1585) when the prospect of a united Netherlands still beckoned. It was the view of a majority of her ministers, throughout those years, and during at least three crises the unanmimous view of all the ministers concerned (including even Burghley), that it was necessary to send immediate and effective aid to the Netherlands. The Queen herself accepted the policy. She professed to regard William as the only salvation of the Netherlands and implicitly accepted his argument that the security and property of England was indissolubly bound with that of the Netherlands. Yet on each occasion, when the moment of decision arrived, she suffered one of her characteristic last-minute blackouts. The onlooker is irresistibly reminded of Churchill's attack on the Baldwin government three and a half centuries later: 'So they go on in strange paradox, decided only to be undecided, resolved to be irresolute, adamant for drift, solid for fluidity, all powerful to be impotent!
Charles Wilson, Queen Elizabeth and the Revolt of the Netherlands, Macmillan, 1970.

Camden gives argument for non-intervention:

These held it the best course if the Queen would meddle no more in matters of the Netherlands, but most strongly fortify her own kingdom, bind the good unto her daily by her innate bounty, restrain the bad, gather money, furnish her navy with all provisions, strengthen the borders towards Scotland with garrisons and maintain the ancient military discipline of England. . . . So would England become impregnable and she on every side most secure and dreadful to her neighbours. . . . But they which were of this opinion incurred heavy displeasure among material men as inclining to the Spaniards' party, degenerate and faint-hearted cowards.
William Camden, Annals of Queen Elizabeth 1615.

This is a forthright attack by a modern historian on Elizabeth's failure to seize the chance presented. It should be contrasted with the view of Camden, a historian who was Elizabeth's contemporary.

Camden lived during Elizabeth's reign and wrote this account soon after her death. It details the less glamorous aims of English foreign policy, which would always be at the back of Elizabeth's mind. Camden was under the patronage of the Cecil family, who would have favoured this cautious appraisal of England's foreign policy needs.

The Duke of Anjou came to the assistance of the rebels in the Netherlands and marched into Antwerp in triumph in 1582. In the following year he lost popularity when his unpaid troops sacked the city. During these years Anjou served Elizabeth's purposes by containing the Spanish army led by Alexander Farnese, Duke of Parma.

The Spanish Ambassador describes the balance of power in the Council:

The bulk of the business depends upon the Queen, Leicester, Walsingham and Cecil, the latter of whom, although he takes part in the resolution of them by virtue of his office, absents himself on many occasions, as he is opposed to the Queen's helping the rebels so effectively and thus weakening her own position. He does not wish to break with Leicester and Walsingham on the matter, they being very much wedded to the States (The Dutch Rebels). . . . They urge the business under cloak of preserving their religion, which Cecil cannot well oppose. . . . Some of the Councillors are well disposed to your Majesty, but Leicester, whose spirit is Walsingham, is so highly favoured with the Queen, notwithstanding his bad character, that he centres in his hands and those of his friends most of the business of the country.

Calendar of State Papers Spanish 1568-1579 (edited by M. Hume), London, 1892.

The Execution of Mary Queen of Scots

Elizabeth had decided in 1568 that she would keep Mary Queen of Scots as a prisoner in England. By this time there was decreasing hope that Elizabeth would be married or have an heir and it became clear that Mary, as next in line to the throne, would be an encouragement to Catholic rebels. Catholic plots against Elizabeth's life recurred with enough regularity for it to be asked whether it would not have been wiser to execute Mary Queen of Scots earlier than 1587 when the punishment was carried out. The most dangerous plot was that of Anthony Babington, a former page, whose plans were carefully monitored by Sir Francis Walsingham. Mary Queen of Scots was deeply involved with Babington. Babington and his conspirators suffered an excruciating traitor's death (20 September 1586) while Mary Queen of Scots was brought to trial (11 October 1587). Elizabeth did all in

Anthony Babington and six of his accomplices were executed in St Giles Fields in September 1586 for their plot with Mary Queen of Scots to depose Elizabeth. Babington had sent Mary Queen of Scots letters in beer barrels while she was imprisoned at Chartley Manor. These were discovered by the government and used as evidence against Mary.

Babington with his Complices in St Giles fields.

her power to avoid carrying out the sentence of the court and finally it was Lord Burghley who risked her wrath by ordering the execution himself (8 February 1587). Was Elizabeth's stance, during the 18 years of Mary's imprisonment in England, bold calculation or timorous indecision? On the side of calculation is the argument that execution of a Queen under human law would justify similar treatment to her by her enemies. There was also the foreign policy implication of Mary's relationship with the French royal family and of her blood relationship with her son James VI, who ruled Scotland. Execution might have disturbed the good relations with France and Scotland, at a time when Elizabeth needed allies against Spain. There is also the need to consider that Philip II of Spain might have been more reluctant to attack England while the main beneficiary would have been the Catholic candidate to the throne, Mary Queen of Scots, whose sympathies were with the French. On the side of timorous indecision is the way that Elizabeth reacted to the events of 1587. She claimed that the decision to execute Mary had been taken by others, even though she had allowed the publication of the court's sentence of death on Mary. Elizabeth either calculated that it was better if she gave the impression that her subordinates had taken matters into their own hands, or she was genuinely indecisive and had not finally made up her mind when the execution took place.

The Queen declines to be pressurized by Parliament:

The Queen's first and second answer to the Petition of Parliament 24 November 1586

1. That her Highness (Elizabeth), moved with some commiseration for the Scottish Queen, in respect of her former dignity and great fortunes in her younger years, her nearness of kindred to her Majesty and also of her sex, could be well pleased to forbear the taking of blood, if, by any other means to be devised by Her Majesty's Great Council of this realm, the safety of her Majesty's person and government might be preserved . . . .

The execution of Mary Queen of Scots in the Hall of Fotheringay Castle in February 1587. Mary Queen of Scots had been a prisoner of Elizabeth for nearly 20 years. When the Dean of Peterborough exhorted her to change her faith, she replied, 'Please, Mr Dean, you have nothing to do with me, nor I with you.'

This passage from D'Ewes's Journal tells of the Queen's answer to Parliament's petition that Mary Queen of Scots should be executed. The Queen was clever at saying 'no' without causing too much offence. Instead of telling them to mind their own business, she gives them an answer answerless.

2. If I should say unto you that I mean not to grant your petition, by my faith I should say unto you more than perhaps I mean. And if I should say unto you I mean to grant your petition, I should then tell you more than is fit for you to know. And thus I deliver to you an answer answerless.

Quoted in G.W. Prothero, *Select Statutes and other Constitutional Documents.*

The French Ambassador pleads for clemency:

God has given your Majesty so many means of defence that even were the said lady

Elizabeth in Parliament. The House of Lords is seated while the House of Commons, led by the Speaker, stand at the bar. The Queen had a long battle with individual commoners to stop them meddling in matters which she thought did not concern them.

This is part of a letter from the French Ambassador Bellièvre to Queen Elizabeth. The King of France, Henry III, was Mary Queen of Scots' brother-in-law and his views needed to be considered, even though expressed through his ambassador. Mary's death would have foreign policy implications; though, in the event, these were insignificant.

(Mary Queen of Scots) free in your dominions, or elsewhere, you would be well guarded, but she imprisoned so strictly, that she could not harm the least of your servants. Scarcely had she completed her twenty-fifth year, when she was first detained as your prisoner . . . which has perhaps rendered it easier for persons to deceive her into malicious snares, intended for her ruin. But if, when she was obeyed in Scotland, as a queen, she had entered your realm in war-like array . . . she could not according to the laws of war, be subjected to harsher treatment than the imposition of a heavy ransom. The said lady entered your realm a persecuted supplicant in every great affliction; she is a princess and your nearest relative; she has been long in hope of being restored to her Kingdom by your goodness and favour; and of all these great hopes, she had no other fruit than perpetual prison . . . .

Quoted in Agnes Strickland, *The Life of Queen Elizabeth*, J.M. Dent, 1906.

Elizabeth was hoping that someone might murder Mary Queen of Scots privately to free her of the responsibility. The decision she was to make was too momentous for her.

In the midst of those doubtful and perplexing thoughts, which so troubled and staggered the Queen's mind, that she gave herself over to solitariness. She sate many times melancholy and mute, and frequently sighing, muttered this to herself, 'aut fer, aut feri', that is, 'either bear with her or smite her', and 'ne feriare feri', – strike, lest thou be stricken.

William Camden, *Annals of Queen Elizabeth 1615*.

Elizabeth blames her council for the decision:

Secretary Wooley wrote this to the Earl of Leicester on 11 February 1587. The Queen had signed the death warrant, but did not want to be held responsible for the execution of Mary Queen of Scots, which had just taken place. Secretary Davison remained in the Tower for 18 months.

It pleaseth her Majesty yesternight to call the Lords and others of her Council before her into her withdrawing chamber where she rebuked us all exceedingly for our concealing from her the proceedings in the Queen of Scots case. But her indignation particularly lighteth upon my Lord Treasurer (Burghley) and Mr Davison . . . . She hath taken order for the committing of Mr Secretary Davison to the Tower . . . .

Quoted in Conyers Read, *Lord Burghley and Queen Elizabeth*.

Elizabeth at War 1585-1603

Elizabeth was a reluctant war leader, since she heartily disliked war. To her a military expedition was no more than an arm of diplomacy aimed to bring the enemy to the negotiating table. Negotiation with Spain continued right up to the departure of the Armada in 1588. Reluctance to spend money on an army and navy that might not be needed led to some under-preparation and under-provisioning of the English forces. Yet Elizabeth must be compared with William Pitt the Younger or Winston Churchill as a war leader who had to withstand a foreign invasion attempt which threatened the whole English way of life.

Historically war leaders have been almost inevitably male and there is no discredit on Elizabeth for not wanting to accompany her armies abroad as her father, Henry VIII, had done in his French campaigns. Her quality as a war leader needs to be considered in relation to the general way in which she chose to fight the war. This will involve a consideration of strategy, general man-management and her choice of leaders.

Elizabeth was surrounded by men who knew or thought they knew how the war could be won. Some of these were sea captains who had earned themselves international reputations for exploits which involved some exploration and trade, and a considerable amount of piracy. The government had managed to discount any official connection with these buccaneers, but privately both the Queen and courtiers took out shares in their expeditions. Sir Francis Drake had become almost a legend in his life-time. The Spanish called him El Draque and it was claimed that he

ÆTATIS SVÆ LVIII
An Dni 1591

Sir John Hawkins (1533-1595) was one of the first Englishmen to try to break the Spaniards' monopoly of trade with their vast overseas empire. He made voyages in 1562, 1564 and 1567. On the third voyage he was subjected to a surprise attack by the Spanish in the bay of St Jean de Uloa. He was later Treasurer of the Navy and was instrumental in providing the Queen with a fleet of 18 galleons.

possessed a magic mirror, through which he could predict his enemies' moves. Another, Sir John Hawkins, had been given the task of providing the Queen with an adequate fleet and he had performed a notable feat in constructing a fleet of galleons, that had qualities of speed and fire power, learnt by someone who had sailed the seas.

The naval threat from Spain increased considerably in 1580 when Philip II became King of both Portugal and Spain. Lisbon in Portugal was a much better port from which to attack England than Cadiz. Philip II already had an army in the Netherlands and needed a deep water port in that area to support his invasion attempt. Naval opinion was that the war could be won by taking the battle to the Spanish bases at Cadiz and Lisbon and by capturing the Spanish treasure fleet that brought silver from the Spanish mines in Peru and Mexico. This silver was used to pay the Italian bankers, who lent Philip II money on its security. The capture of a treasure fleet would bring riches to the Queen and bankruptcy to Spain in one glorious action.

Cautionary town: a town given as
security.

Elizabeth's view was that the navy's role was to guard the Channel and
that the task was to deprive the Spanish of deep water ports in the Channel
area. Her strategy in the Netherlands therefore was to keep her small army
near to the port of Flushing, which she had also been given as a cautionary
town – as it was the nearest deep water port to the Spanish army. Later in
the war she took similar measures to stop the Spanish gaining control of a
French port on the north coast of Brittany. Elizabeth also paid attention to
Ireland as the Catholic Irish lords were always likely to befriend the
Spanish cause and Philip II could use it as a back door into England.

Elizabeth found herself fighting the war on at least four fronts – the sea,
the Netherlands, France and Ireland. She was dependent on money that
could be raised from taxation, short-term loans raised at Antwerp, loans
from the City or sales of crown land. Given her limited resources, she was
always looking for the cheapest ways of waging war. Expeditions to fight
Spain became business ventures with shareholders; armies had to be
disbanded as soon as their usefulness had ended and reliance had to be
placed on allies. Her French ally Henry IV thought that he was being
duped by the Queen and referred admiringly to how Elizabeth 'made war
at this time so cheaply against so great an enemy . . .' Maurice of Nassau,
William the Silent's son, might have felt the same in the Netherlands.

The strongest criticism that could be made of Elizabeth in her war policy
was her choice of leaders. It was traditional that the leadership of armies
would be placed in the hands of the Queen's peers or tenants in chief and
it was possible to choose competent leaders from this source. Peregrine
Bertie, Lord Willoughby, her second choice in the Netherlands and Charles
Blount, Lord Mountjoy, her second choice in Ireland, both proved
extremely competent. It might be said that on each first occasion
Elizabeth's faith was misplaced in one of her favourites. Neither the Earl of
Leicester in the Netherlands nor the Earl of Essex in Ireland proved worthy
of her trust.

An English galleon, the Ark Royal.
*Elizabeth purchased this ship from
Raleigh and it became the flagship at the
time of the Armada. This ship, like all
galleons, was a fast-sailing and
manoeuvrable fighting ship with great
broadside gun power.*

Leicester in the Netherlands 1585-1588

The war with Spain started in 1585 when Elizabeth sent a small army under Leicester to aid Maurice of Nassau. In the previous year not only had Maurice's father, William the Silent, been assassinated, but also Elizabeth's former suitor, the Duke of Anjou, died. Military intervention was only intended as a defensive measure to stop the whole of the Low Countries falling under Spanish control and Elizabeth refused the offer of sovereignty over the northern provinces. She chose the Earl of Leicester as the commander of the army in the Netherlands, who had long favoured a war policy against Spain. Leicester had remained Elizabeth's favourite since her accession and took part in the elaborate platonic flirtations which Elizabeth enjoyed, with the nickname 'Eyes' and pet name 'Robin'.

Within a few weeks of his arrival in the Netherlands, Leicester infuriated the Queen by accepting the title and office of governor-general from the northern rebels, which associated Elizabeth with Spain's enemy in a way she had wished to avoid. Her fury at his disobedience and insensitivity led to a breakdown in the relationship, which left Leicester feeling rather isolated. It seems that Elizabeth knew the kind of military leader who was needed as she sent with Leicester Sir John Norris, who was a professional soldier with plenty of experience of warfare in Ireland. Leicester did not possess the leadership qualities to make use of Norris's talents and it became difficult to justify the choice of Leicester as leader. He returned to England in November 1586, but was sent back with a fresh army seven months later. Elizabeth must therefore take full blame for Leicester's short-comings.

Elizabeth scolds Leicester:

What availeth wit when it fails the owner at greatest need? Do that you are bidden and leave your considerations for your own affairs . . . . I am assured of your dutiful thoughts, but I am utterly at squares with this childish dealing.
Quoted in J.E. Neale, *Queen Elizabeth.*

Elizabeth scolds the Earl of Leicester for accepting the sovereignty of the northern provinces. She allowed Leicester to keep the title but held a grudge against him.

Leicester is kept short of advice by Elizabeth:

I have let my lords (of the Council) here understand how unkindly your lordship taketh it that you hear so seldom from them, and that since your charge there you never received any letter of advice from them. They answer, as it is truth, that, her Majesty retaining the whole direction of the causes of that country to herself and such advice as she receiveth underhand, they knew not what to write or advise. She can by no means . . . endure that the causes of that country should be subject to any debate in Council, otherwise than as she herself shall direct, and therefore men forbear to do that which other wise they would.
Correspondence of Robert Dudley, Earl of Leicester (edited by J. Bruce), Camden Society, 1844.

Walsingham wrote this to Leicester in April 1586. The Queen was in charge of Netherlands affairs, but Leicester received no advice. The Queen would not even allow the matter to be discussed. Can Elizabeth therefore be blamed for Leicester's poor performance?

These two things being so contrary to Her Majesty's disposition, the one that it breedeth the doubt of a perpetual war, the other for that it ever requireth an increase of charges do marvellously distract her and make her repent that ever she did enter the action.
Correspondence of Robert Dudley, Earl of Leicester (edited by J. Bruce).

Walsingham wrote this to Leicester in July 1586. It mentioned two important considerations for Elizabeth. She did not want perpetual war and she feared the cost of war.

Sir John Norris proves uncooperative

Norris will so dissemble, so crouch and so cunningly carry his doings as no man living would imagine that there were half the malice or vindictive mind that doth plainly his deeds prove to be . . . . Since the loss of Grave [at which Norris was wounded and after which he was knighted by Leicester, April 1586], he is as coy and as strange to give any counsel or any advice as if he were a mere stranger to us.
Correspondence of Robert Dudley, Earl of Leicester (edited by J. Bruce).

Leicester wrote this to Walsingham concerning Walsingham's cousin John Norris, who had a command in the Netherlands. Norris is obviously not being very helpful to Leicester. In fact he is being positively uncooperative.

The Singeing of the King of Spain's Beard

Sir Francis Drake attacked the Spanish fleet that was being assembled in Cadiz harbour on 29 April 1587 and forced Philip II to delay the dispatch of the Armada by one year. Drake succeeded in humiliating the Spanish by taking control of the port for 24 hours and escaping, even though he was becalmed in the mouth of the harbour for 12 hours. Drake claimed to have sunk, burnt or captured 37 Spanish ships and destroyed considerable material being prepared for the Armada. He then occupied Cape St Vincent for a month, using it as a base to prevent the assembly of the Spanish fleet. This expedition demonstrated how successfully well-directed aggression could be used against the Spanish Empire, and it does raise the question of the Queen's timidity. Some have claimed that the Queen intended to call off the expedition, but was foiled by Drake's prompt departure. An alternative explanation could be that the Queen supported the expedition wholeheartedly, but wanted to give the impression to Spain

Sir Francis Drake (1540-1596) shown with Hondius's map indicating his voyage round the world 1577-80. This incursion into the Spanish Empire was unofficial, but the Queen had a financial interest in the venture.

These instructions were described three weeks after Drake had left in a letter from Walsingham to Sir Edward Stafford, the English ambassador in France. Stafford was thought to be passing information on to Mendoza, the former Spanish ambassador in England, and thus it would reach Spain. Walsingham gave the impression that Drake had been forbidden to enter any Spanish ports. Why should he give this kind of information to Stafford unless he expected him to pass it on?

These were the Queen's countermanding orders which never reached Drake. The Queen made clear she drew back from open warfare in the hope that Philip II and she could reach a peaceful solution. Was it timidity or was it an attempt to bluff the Spanish?

Drake seems grateful to Elizabeth and ready for instructions on 24 May 1587. There is no hint of lack of faith in the Queen's real intention or regret at what he had done at Cadiz, against the Queen's wishes.

that Drake was acting beyond his instructions.

Drake's instructions:

To impeach the joining together of the King of Spain's fleet out of their several ports, to keep victuals from them, to follow them in case they should come forward towards England or Ireland and to cut off as many as he could and impeach their landing as also to set up such as should either come out of the West or East Indies into Spain or go out of Spain thither.

Quoted in Conyers Read, *Mr Secretary Walsingham and the Policy of Elizabeth.*

Elizabeth's countermanding orders:

Forbear to enter forcibly into any of the said King's ports or havens or to offer violence to any of his towns or shipping within harbouring or to do any act of hostility upon the land. And yet . . . you should do your best endeavour (avoiding as much as may lie in you the effusion of Christian blood) to get into your possession such shipping of the said King or his subjects as you shall find as sea.

Quoted in Garrett Mattingley, *The Defeat of the Spanish Armada, Cape, 1959.*

Drake reports confidently from the Portuguese coast:

As long as it shall please God to give us provisions to eat and drink and that our ships and wind and weather will permit us, you shall surely hear of us near this Cape of Vincent where we do and will expect daily what her Majesty and your honours will further command.

God make us thankful that her Majesty sent out these few ships in time.

If there were 6 more of her Majesty's good ships of the second sort, we should be better able to keep their forces from joining . . . .

Garrett Mattingly, *The Defeat of the Spanish Armada.*

The knighting of Sir Francis Drake on board the Golden Hind *in April 1581. The painting is historically incorrect as it was in fact the French ambassador who dubbed Sir Francis and not the Queen.*

The Spanish Armada sailed up the Channel in a crescent formation with the English fleet in close attendance. The Spanish progress up the Channel turned into a nine day running battle.

The Armada

The situation in 1588 was similar to that of 1587. Once again Philip II had prepared a fleet to invade England and once again Elizabeth and Lord Burghley were attempting to negotiate a settlement. Drake offered his services to carry the war to the Spanish coast, but the offer was refused. Elizabeth had a fleet of galleons constructed under the eye of Sir John Hawkins, which were to prove themselves superior to the slower, bulkier Spanish ships. There seemed plenty of confidence that the Spanish attack would be contained and this was reflected in the Queen's speech to the troops assembled at Tilbury. Once the threat of invasion had passed and the Spanish fleet was making its way home round the north of the British Isles, Burghley was quick to begin the demobilization. Some councillors at the time and some modern commentators more recently have criticized Elizabeth for her unpreparedness and for her lack of commitment to a continuation of the war, though this is consistent with Elizabeth's war strategy. Her critics would say that she trusted too much in her luck.

Drake offers to lead an expedition to Spain:

This was a letter from Francis Drake to the Queen written on 28 April 1588. It shows a good understanding of the Queen's war strategy.

If a good peace be not forthwith concluded, then these great preparations of the Spaniard may be speedily prevented as much as in your majesty lieth, by sending your forces to encounter them somewhat far off, and more near their own coast, which will be the better cheap for your majesty and people and much the dearer for the enemy.

Quoted in John Barrow, *Life of Drake*, London, 1843.

This picture shows the various ways in which the English met the threat from the Armada. The beacons warned that the Spanish were near, the army was prepared to meet them, and the English fire ships disturbed the Spanish ships at their anchorage in the Channel. The lower picture shows people giving thanks for the delivery from danger.

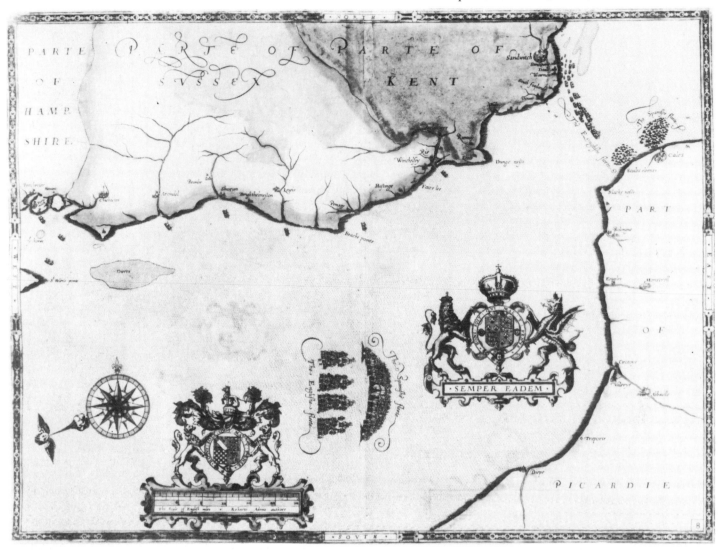

This map shows the fleets moving up the Channel and the Spanish ships anchored off the French coast. The English fleets defend the Straits of Dover. The English commader, Lord Howard of Effingham, sent in eight fire ships which forced the tight Spanish formation to break up. Most of the Spanish ships cut their anchors and drifted away. The resulting break-up of the Spanish formation helped to give the English fleet a victory on the following day that put the Armada to flight and ended the threat of invasion.

Walsingham complains at the lack of preparation:

I am sorry to see so great a danger hanging over this realm so slightly regarded and so carelessly provided for . . . . Seeing we have neither recourse to pray nor to such effectual preparations as the danger importeth . . . .
Quoted in Conyers Read, *Mr Secretary Walsingham and the Policy of Elizabeth.*

Walsingham wrote this to Lord Burghley in June 1588 when peace negotiations continued beyond the time that the Armada had sailed.

Elizabeth speaks to her troops at Tilbury:

The speech was delivered by Elizabeth to her troops at Tilbury on 18 August 1588. The Armada was in flight by the time, but people in England weren't yet certain the danger was over, and Elizabeth's speech caught the mood of national unity. Parma was Alexander Farnese, Duke of Parma, Spanish governor of the Netherlands — the greatest general of the age.

My loving people, we have been persuaded of our safety, to take heed how we commit ourself to armed multitudes for fear of treachery; but I assure you, I do not desire to live to distrust my faithful and loving people. Let tyrants fear. I have always so behaved myself, that under God, I have placed my chiefest strength and safeguard in the loyal hearts and good wills of my subjects, and therefore I am come amongst you as you see, at this time, not for my recreation and disport, but being resolved, in the midst and heat of the battle, to live or die amongst you all, and to lay down for my God and for my kingdom, and for my people, my honour and my blood even in the dust. I know I have the body of a weak and feeble woman, but I

Elizabeth at Tilbury in 1588. She made an inspection of all her troops (according to Camden there were 3000), saying that she needed no guard among fellow countrymen in arms for her service. The Queen rode a white gelding and was dressed all in white herself. On the next day there was a review, a march past and a famous speech from Elizabeth.

have the heart and stomach of a king, and of a king of England too, and I think foul scorn that Parma or Spain, or any prince of Europe should dare to invade the borders of my realm . . . .
Quoted in Garrett Mattingley, *The Defeat of the Spanish Armada.*

Burghley lays down rules for spending:

To spend in time convenient is wisdom
To continue charges without needful cause bringeth repentance
To hold on charges without knowledge of the certainty thereof and the means to support them is lack of wisdom.
Quoted in Conyers Read, *Lord Burghley and Queen Elizabeth.*

Written by Lord Burghley on 12 August 1588 as his rules for justified expenditure. The problem of finance always haunted Lord Burghley as Lord Treasurer and the Queen was mindful of this too.

Sixtus V praises Elizabeth:

She certainly is a great Queen and were she only a Catholic she would be our dearly beloved. Just look how well she governs! She is only a woman, only mistress of half an island, and yet she makes herself feared by Spain, by France, by the Empire, by all.
Quoted in J.E. Neale, *Queen Elizabeth.*

This was an unsolicited testimonial from the Pope, Sixtus V, who admired Elizabeth, even though she was his enemy.

The Earl of Essex (1566-1601) was an important figure in Elizabeth's last years. He joined the Portugal Expedition 1589, was given a command at Rouen in 1591, commanded a very successful raid on Cadiz in 1596, went to the Azores in 1597, but lost his reputation during his command in Ireland 1598. He was executed for leading a rebellion in 1601.

Elizabeth and Essex

Essex was the step-son of Leicester and became the Queen's favourite after Leicester's death in 1588. At 23, he was young enough to be treated not only as a favourite, but perhaps also as the son Elizabeth had never had. Elizabeth found it difficult not to grant Essex his wishes and Essex was clever enough to use his position and influence to advantage. He gained popularity by his dashing involvement in warfare on land and sea, and his connection with some notable exploits such as the attack on Cadiz in 1596. He developed his own diplomatic network so that he could challenge Lord Burghley and his son Robert as the purveyors of sound advice to the Queen. Worst of all, he was willing to question the authority of the Queen both in public and private. His downfall began with his insistence that he should lead the Queen's army into Ireland in 1599. Failure there and subsequent indiscretion led to his disgrace and involvement in a plot to overthrow the Queen and seize control of the court. He was executed in 1601.

Bacon's advice to Essex:

'A man of a nature not to be ruled; that hath the advantage of my affection and

Bacon starts by analysing the Queen's thoughts on Essex and then warns Essex of the danger that he is in after the Cadiz victory in 1596.

knoweth it; of an estate not grounded to his greatness; of a popular reputation; of a military dependence.' I demand whether there can be a more dangerous image than this presented to any monarch living, much more to a lady, and of her Majesty's apprehension.
Quoted in J.E. Neale, *Queen Elizabeth*.

Essex expresses his fury to Elizabeth:

This was Essex's reaction to receiving a cuff round the ear after he had turned his back on the Queen in anger at being told that Sir William Knollys would be leader of the army in Ireland.

This is an outrage that I will not put up with. I would not have borne it from your father's hands.
Quoted in Lytton Strachey, *Elizabeth and Essex*, Chatto and Windus, 1928; Penguin, 1950.

Essex refuses to return to court

This letter was written by Essex to Lord Keeper Egerton, explaining why he was staying away from court after the humiliating ear-boxing. Notice that he begins to discuss the limits of royal power.

The indissoluble duty which I owe to her Majesty is only the duty of allegiance, which I never will, nor never can, fail in. The duty of attendance is no indissoluble duty . . . . When the vilest of all indignities is done to me, doth religion enforce me to sue? Doth God require it? Is it impiety not to do it? What, cannot princes err? Cannot subjects receive wrong? Is an earthly power or authority infinite?
Lives and Letters of the Devereux, Earls of Essex (edited by W.B. Devereux).

Essex finally had his way and was appointed as Lord Deputy of Ireland. There was no great competition for this difficult post and many courtiers were glad to think that Essex was going to what the Venetian ambassador called 'the Englishman's grave'. In a round about way it became Essex's grave too. Tyrone was Hugh O'Neill, Earl of Tyrone, who ruled Ulster.

Essex gets his way:

I have beaten Knollys and Mountjoy in the Council and by God I will beat Tyrone in the field.
Quoted in J.E. Neale, *Queen Elizabeth*.

Conclusion

Elizabeth's aim was to give England a long period of stability after the rapid changes in religion and land ownership that had occurred in the middle of the sixteenth century. Her longevity coupled with her conservatism enabled her to achieve this, but in the process she frustrated the development of a governmental system and Church which would be acceptable to the emerging gentry class. Her Church did not reflect the spirituality of some of her leading citizens nor did the parliament as operated by Elizabeth give them a place for open expression of their aspirations.

Elizabeth's regime depended too much on herself and not only did it run down as she became older, but it could not be operated by a king who lacked her personal skills. One had to admire her dedication to her job, her skill in using the Privy Council as a nerve centre of government, and her formation of a court group or party which retained a remarkable cohesion for most of her reign. The system began to creak as it sought to administer and finance the long war at the end of her reign. There was disagreement within the Council about how the war with the Spanish should be fought and Spain continued to present an invasion threat. The government resorted to short-term expedients like tax-farming, the sale of offices and

Hardwick Hall. This is a good example of a great house built in Elizabeth's reign. It was constructed between 1591 and 1597 by Elizabeth, Countess of Shrewsbury (Bess of Hardwick), who became wealthy as a result of her four marriages. E S in the roof decoration stands for Elizabeth Shrewsbury, who built the house to her own glory.

Yeoman House. This house at Minster in Kent is typical of the better housing that was being built by the richer farmers in Elizabeth's reign. Elizabeth's reign was a time of rebuilding of all kinds, showing the confidence of the age.

the granting of monopolies to reward government supporters, at a time when there was never enough money to finance the war. At court there was a split between the Cecils and the Essex faction for control of the court and government. This kind of struggle for control of the centre of government and its fruits had been the source of civil disturbance in France during most of Elizabeth's reign, and it was no surprise that it should end with Essex's attack on the city in 1601. Luckily Essex attempted his *coup d'état* when he was already discredited, but his former popularity had been such that with better calculation he might really have seized control of the centres of power.

The Queen cannot be blamed for getting older nor should she be ridiculed for attempting to win a reputation for eternal youth. Yet it needs to be considered whether the regime would not have been stronger had she provided for the succession more clearly. Her pledge to remain a Virgin suggests that she did not want marriage or children herself. She therefore must have been continually concerned, as her councillors were, that the stability of England depended on her own continued existence. While Mary Queen of Scots lived, the probability was that Elizabeth's death would be followed by disputes over Mary's right or fitness to succeed. Historians should not therefore be duped into thinking that her regime had a rock-like stability or that the Protestant succession of James I was inevitable. Much had been left to chance.

Elizabeth's moderation in religion has been questioned, but due regard must be paid to the dangers that she faced. It is much easier to be tolerant in peacetime than in war. It is fair therefore, to assess whether Elizabeth's attitude to religious non-conformity changed with the approach of war. Measures to stifle possible enemy agents are far more excusable when war is imminent or in progress. Note should be taken of the execution of several Puritan leaders of more independent mind soon after the Armada, as well as the 183 Catholics who died.

Elizabeth's reputation for indecision has been illustrated from many aspects, but for a balanced view many more examples ought to be

The Elizabethan Theatre. This is a performance at the Swan Theatre in the time of Shakespeare. During Elizabeth's reign the theatre flourished, even though the Puritans did not like it. The Swan Theatre on the south bank of the Thames had space for 3000 people and was the largest and most distinguished theatre in London, though not as famous as The Globe.

William Camden (1551-1623) was the first historian of Elizabeth's reign. He was also a topographer, giving a description of England in his book Britannia. *He was a schoolmaster who became headmaster of Westminster.*

considered. It was never Elizabeth's wish to change things. It was her intention to learn to live with problems rather than to solve them. She therefore reacted to events only when a vital interest was involved. Her decision-making therefore needs to be seen in relation to her total strategy and her total strategy needs to be assessed from some appraisal of the national interest. There is no point in making a hasty decision, unless the issue is immediate and important. What we do know is that some of her ministers, especially Walsingham and Leicester, thought that the Queen was dangerously over-cautious.

Her success in the war against Spain was a notable triumph, especially when the population and resources of England and Spain are compared. The war techniques of the time ensured that it was easier to defend than to attack. Elizabeth's concentration on defence coupled with the possession of ocean-going ships which were much faster and manoeuvrable than those of Spain was the key to her success. The brilliance of individual feats such as Drake's attack on Cadiz owe more to individual flair than to Elizabeth's leadership, though the loyalty of Drake to the Queen was a notable factor. The disposition of armies in the Netherlands, Brittany and Ireland must not be forgotten. It was a war involving the whole of the Western Atlantic area and when an English army did face the Spanish at Kinsale in 1601, Lord Mountjoy, Elizabeth's general, won a notable victory and accepted the capitulation of the Spanish army.

Elizabeth sought to bring England stability and to a large extent she succeeded. The confidence and wealth of her subjects was expressed in great rebuilding. William Camden the historian was also a topographer who described the countryside in his great book *Britannia*, showing a new national pride in England as a noteworthy and important country. Elizabeth's courtiers and nobles felt wealthy and secure enough to patronize artists, dramatists, musicians and poets. Their achievement is still judged to be a high point in English creativity and consideration must be given to whether it was Elizabeth who provided the climate for their success. Alternatively it might be ascribed to factors like better education, the stimulus of Italian ideas or the richness of the English language.

If the success of the reign is attributed to a stable society and a growing economy, then Elizabeth's policies had worked. Yet she had not satisfied the political and spiritual aspirations of those who were benefiting from increased wealth and a better education. It is their dissatisfaction and alienation from the court that contributed to open opposition in the reign of James I and a Civil War between Crown and Parliament in the reign of Charles I. If reform is frustrated in one reign, then the frustration is likely to be expressed in the next. Was this the price of Elizabeth's achievement?

Elizabeth's Contemporaries

Burghley, William Cecil, Lord (1520-1598). He became Elizabeth's chief secretary of state in 1558. Given the title Lord in 1571 and in 1572 was made Lord Treasurer – a position he held until his death. Thus Elizabeth's chief minister for 40 years.

Drake, Sir Francis (1540-1596). Commanded a ship on John Hawkins's expedition 1567 and present at St Jean d'Uloa, 1568. Attacked the Spanish treasure train at Nombre di Dios 1572. Sailed round the world 1577-78. Attacked Cadiz 1587. Helped defeat Armada 1588. Took part in Portugal Expedition 1589. Died at Porto Bello in Caribbean in 1596.

Essex, Robert Devereux, Earl of (1566-1601). Step-son of the Earl of Leicester. Favourite of Elizabeth. Soldier who fought in Netherlands and France. Challenged domination of Cecils at Elizabeth's court. Took part in successful Cadiz expedition 1596. Had unsuccessful command as Lord Lieutenant of Ireland and lost favour. Took part in rebellion 1601 and was executed.

Leicester, Robert Dudley, Earl of (1532?-1588). Favourite of the Queen. Made Master of the Horse, Knight of the Garter, a Privy Councillor and given an earldom. Involved in the scandal surrounding the mysterious death of his first wife, Amy, in 1560. Elizabeth wanted him to marry Mary Queen of Scots in 1563. Married the widow of the Earl of Essex 1578. Commanded the expedition to the Netherlands in 1585.

Mary Stuart, Queen of Scots (1542-87). Queen of France as wife of Francis II 1559-1560. Returned to rule Scotland. Was keen to be recognized as successor to Elizabeth. Married twice more, first to Lord Darnley, who was murdered 1567 and then to the Earl of Bothwell. Faced noble rebellion, was forced to abdicate and was imprisoned. Escaped to England in 1568 and was held as a prisoner until her execution in 1587.

Philip II, King of Spain (1527-1598). Married Mary Tudor in 1554 and succeeded his father, Charles V, as King of Spain in 1556. He worked hard to centralise his possessions on Madrid and became increasingly interested in destroying Protestantism in England and the Netherlands. He was involved in open war with Elizabeth from 1585 onwards and dispatched the Spanish Armada in 1588.

Raleigh, Sir Walter (1552-1618). Courtier, explorer, scholar and colonizer. Established a colony in Ireland and tried to establish colonies in America. Introduced potatoes and tobacco to England. Favoured continuation of war with Spain. Under James I he was imprisoned and executed to please Spain.

Walsingham, Sir Francis (1536-1589). Succeeded Burghley as Secretary of State in 1573. Acted as ambassador to Scotland, France and the Netherlands. Favoured war policy against Spain. Ringed Mary Queen of Scots with spies and unearthed Babington plot.

William the Silent, Prince of Orange (1533-1584). Opposed the oppressive policy of Philip II in the Netherlands. Held lands in France, Germany and Holland, but became the champion of the Protestant Northern Provinces of the Netherlands in their resistance to the Spanish army. Sought the alliance of Elizabeth, but he was assassinated in 1584 before the alliance with England was achieved in 1585.

Book List

Bindoff, S.T., *Tudor England*, Pelican, 1952.

Black, J.B., *The Reign of Elizabeth*, O.U.P., 1936.

Bruce, John, *Correspondence of Robert Dudley, Earl of Leicester*, Camden Society Series 1 Vol. 27, 1844.

Calendar of State Papers Foreign, (ed.) J. Stevenson, London, 1961-65.

Calendar of State Papers Spanish, (ed.) M. Hume 1558-99, London, 1892.

Calendar of State Papers Venetian, Rawdon Brown & G.C. Bentinck, London, 1890.

Camden, William, *Annals of Queen Elizabeth 1615*, London, 1635.

Devereux, W.B., *Lives and Letters of the Devereux Earls of Essex*, London, 1853.

Dodd, R.H., *Life in Elizabethan England*, Batsford, 1961.

Elton, G.R., *England under the Tudors*, Methuen, 1965.

Elton, G.R., *The Tudor Constitution*, C.U.P., 1960.

Hentzner, Paul, *Travels in England in the Reign of Queen Elizabeth*, Cassell, 1884.

Holinshed, Raphael, *Chronicles of England, Scotland and Ireland 1587*, London, 1803.

Fletcher, Anthony, *Tudor Rebellions*, Longmans, 1968.

Frazer, N.L., *English History in Contemporary Poetry No 111*, Historical Association, 1970.

Froude, J.A., *History of England 12 volumes*, Longmans, 1893.

Jenkins, Elizabeth, *Elizabeth and Leicester*, Victor Gollancz, 1961.

Lettenhove, Kervyn de, *Rélations Politiques des Pays Bas et L'Angleterre 11 volumes*, Brussels, 1888-1900.

McCaffrey, Wallace, *Queen Elizabeth and the Making of Policy 1572-88*, Princeton, 1981.

Mattingley, Garrett, *The Defeat of the Spanish Armada*, Cape 1959, Pelican, 1962.

McGrath, Patrick, *Papists and Puritans under Elizabeth I*, Blandford, 1967.

Morris, Christopher, *The Tudors*, Batsford 1955, Fontana 1966.

Neale, J.E., *Queen Elizabeth I*, Cape 1934, Pelican, 1960.

Neale, J.E., *Elizabeth and her Parliaments 1559-81*, Cape, 1953.

Neale, J.E., *Elizabeth and her Parliaments 1581-1601*, Cape, 1957.

Prothero, G.W., *Statutes and Constitutional Documents 1558-1625*, O.U.P., 1894.

Read, Conyers, *Mr Secretary Cecil and Queen Elizabeth*, Cape, 1955.

Read, Conyers, *Lord Burghley and Queen Elizabeth*, Cape, 1960.

Rowse, A.L., *The Elizabethan Renaissance*, Cardinal, 1971.

Rowse, A.L., *The England of Elizabeth*, Macmillan, 1950.

Strachey, Lytton, *Elizabeth and Essex*, Chatto and Windus, 1928.

Strickland, Agnes, *The Life of Elizabeth*, J.M. Dent, 1906.

Smith, J.C., Selincourt, E. de. *The Poetical Works of Edmund Spenser*, O.U.P., 1912.

Tanner, J.R., *Constitutional Documents 1485-1603*, C.U.P., 1940.

Wilson, Charles, *Queen Elizabeth and the Revolt of the Netherlands*, Macmillan, 1970.

Index